WHEREVER WE GO, THERE WE ARE

WESLEY BRANN

Wherever We Go, There We Are

Copyright © 2018 by Wesley Brann

Published by Clay Bridges in Houston, TX
www.ClayBridgesPress.com

All rights reserved. No part of this publication may be reproduced, stored in a retrieval system, or transmitted in any form by any means, electronic, mechanical, photocopy, recording, or otherwise, without the prior permission of the publisher, except as provided for by USA copyright law.

ISBN-10: 1-63296-312-4
ISBN-13: 978-1-63296-312-3
eISBN-10: 1-63296-282-9
eISBN-13: 978-1-63296-282-9

Front cover author headshot copyright © 2018 Bethany Brann

Special Sales: Most Clay Bridges titles are available in special quantity discounts. Custom imprinting or excerpting can also be done to fit special needs. Contact Clay Bridges at Info@ClayBridgesPress.com.

"Beautifully written and inspirational, in its rawest form, Wesley has shared about his life from his upbringing, to his addictions, to his failures and relapses, and to his road of recovery. Wesley has captured every emotion behind his thought process to help us understand what goes on in an addict's head. He also conveys that although it is extremely difficult and may take several attempts to become sober, if you put trust in yourself and the Lord, anything is possible. Wesley is a prime example of someone who has turned his life around 180 degrees and is still continuing to better himself while living a much happier life."

—**Michelle V. Pepping**

"In *Wherever We Go, There We Are* by Wesley Brann, I developed a sense that there is hope in anyone. One of the many things that I found myself liking was the raw emotion told by the author through true events, outrageous humor, and heartfelt scenes that had me reading more. The most attention-grabbing part would be that the same man who wrote this is the same man who is always joking, sweating, and bossing me around. Truly motivational and recommended for any and everyone! Be prepared to scratch the surface of Wesley Brann's life. Proud of you."

—**Alain Man**,
UTD student

"I've known Wes Brann all of his life through a deep friendship with his remarkable parents, so I've had a frequently very painful front-row seat as Wes has been through the trials and tribulations of more than 20 years of battling addiction and mental illness. His totally authentic and transparent (and very witty) sharing of his years of a revolving door of to-hell-and-back-and-back-again battle, and his blunt, honest, and practical insights and wisdom about the challenges of trying to live just one day at a time and to sustain recovery, are an absolute must read for anyone mired in the despair of the black hole of addiction and mental illness; and also for friends and family, and really anyone who is struggling to understand these very disabling and insidious diseases that continue to damage and destroy so many. I highly recommend *Wherever We Go, There We Are* as a wonderful 'hope manual,' and I'm grateful for Wes's courageous willingness to bare his struggle and suffering as an offering of hope for his fellow sufferers and their families and friends."

—**Rev. Jim Turley**,
United Methodist Pastor

This book is dedicated to my father. For he may be my biggest fan, let the records show that I am his. And to my mother— for believing in me when I didn't believe in myself. And for the addict who has woken up face down in his or her own vomit . . . I am one of you.

Wesley Brann

TABLE OF CONTENTS

Introduction	1
Chapter 1: The Educational Part	3
Chapter 2: Crazy Does It	11
Chapter 3: The Story	20
Chapter 4: Admitted	41
Chapter 5: The World Through My Eyes	49
Chapter 6: Wesley's Cube	52
Chapter 7: The Deadly Combination	56
Chapter 8: Switch Hitting—One Addiction for Another	61
Chapter 9: Stuck in a Funk	65
Chapter 10: Undoing the Wrongs	69
Chapter 11: The Trifecta—Addiction, Bipolar, and Cancer	74
Chapter 12: The Last Chapter	81
Philosophy According to Dick, by Wesley Brann	89
"Me, Myself, & about I", A Biography Trailer	141
Notes	143

INTRODUCTION

If you've bought, borrowed, or stole this book, thank you. The contents within are not designed to keep you sober. Everything you will read is what I needed or used to keep myself sober and relatively sane. But if along the journey, some parts relate to what you've experienced, have seen in others, or if you know someone who has started walking down the wrong path, then it's time to do something about it. My writings and any other type of book will only do so much.

The whole concept of this book is to let some of you out there relate to, experience, and understand what alcohol, drugs and mental health beliefs have done to this hopeless drunk. If you are not a drunk of my caliber or don't personally deal with dual diagnosis, then reading this material may help someone else in your life you really care about. Do not lose hope and never quit caring or trying. The solution is out there. It just takes different strokes for different folks.

I originally wrote this to help me and only me. It was a personal project that turned into an awareness project. I wanted it to get out to the brothers and sisters in recovery. There are too many books on how to stay sober and I noticed that there is no flexibility on how to do it. If you need help, search for it. If you need a helping hand, ask for it. And if you need a meeting, look for one. The obvious is the obvious. This book is not hard or long reading. It is not complicated, so don't make it that way. This is just one addict telling you how life went on—whether I was sober, drunk, depressed, dealing with cancer, or all the above at once. So sit back, relax, and drink your overpriced coffee. If you get anything out of this book, use it for your sobriety. If not, well it can be used as a coaster or a place to hide your money!

CHAPTER 1
THE EDUCATIONAL PART

Gina Davis made a statement in the movie, *The Fly* that went a little something like this, "Be afraid. Be very afraid." How many people in this world live like that in one form or another? Fear has a tendency to prevent us from doing things that we either want to do, or need to do. Some people are afraid of spiders, while others are afraid of success. Then there are those who are flat out afraid of the whole spectrum. These people are called addicts or alcoholics. I know, I'm part of the brotherhood that covers both. I say this because I am afraid of spiders, just one type though, and I do have a fear of success. Fear can mean either two things: Face everything and recover, or fuck everything and run. How many times have you done the latter of the two? I have, many, many times.

Because of the wreckage of our past, once we do get into recovery and gain some sobriety via treatment centers or regular meetings, we begin to wonder what will happen down the line. Our future, our unknown, has and will driven us back into the trenches for further misery. It is at this point we find a fellow member or sponsor, and explain in detail what is going on in our head. We cannot sit on it, nor can we fix it alone. The fact that it is difficult to understand that we cannot control the future, but instead must focus and remain in today, is the greatest understatement of the year. My problem with this was: "What about my bills?" "What about my house or marriage?" "Will I be able to work in a great job?" Honestly, if you stop and think about it, does it really matter?

So often in addiction do we give away relationships, employment, responsibilities, and material objects without a second thought. Now we get a little time sober under our belt and all of a sudden, we want to take on the world. Relax. Take it slowly. If we follow this spiritual program a hundred percent, then we will gain ten times what we were originally looking for. It is a little early to be discussing spirituality, but as you read ahead, you will find a more in-depth chapter on God.

If you have had a taste for AA and its meetings, then you have heard the phrase, "Let go and let God." As addicts, we have a fear of letting something greater than us run the show. We like to be in control of everything we do. By letting go and accepting the suggestions of our brotherhood that a power greater than ourselves can make life better, we will know a peace that we never had that will guide us along a spiritual journey through the steps of Alcoholics Anonymous.

But if anyone had an experience like I did, and once again took back the reigns and said, "Thanks for getting me this far, I'll take it from here!" then you know the repercussions. We once again dig our own grave. Our thinking is due to complacency or apathy because we shuffle our priorities and lose track of what we need to do. We are slaves to self-will. The more self-absorbed we become, the more fear there is.

In my case, I didn't necessarily see the fear there because I thought I did away with it all on my fourth step. It turns out there were underlying factors of inner fear I had not dealt with, such as abandonment issues surrounding my biological father, success in the simplest form, being able to truly love myself, and so on. As a result, within a certain amount of time, I was drunk all over again, pounding my head against the wall and trying to figure out what had happened.

But I learned. I learned that love liberates fear by working the twelve steps daily and understanding the four disciplines of love. The first one is to be dedicated to the truth. This means that no matter what the circumstances may be, honesty is the best policy. Be honest to yourself, your family, and all those around you. Believe me when I say that if you aren't, even if you think it is something small, you have just put a halt to your spiritual program.

Next, accept responsibility for your actions. We are quick to blame loved ones, the legal system, employers, and everyday situations. Why not? It is easier to do so. So we must sever this blaming and finger pointing process if we are wanting to grow. In the beginning, it will most likely be hard for the newcomer because of fear. But with anything else, in time, this process will become easier and easier. It will take practice. No one is perfect, so don't think you will be cured of self-will and run riot, my friend. Our brothers and sisters with long-term sobriety lie as well, we all do, but the difference is that if they are working a solid program, they catch themselves and either correct their mistake on the spot, or after going through the tenth through twelfth-step management process at night, they correct it the next day. This is an acceptable goal to work toward.

Third is delaying gratification. We want, want, want it, and we want it right now! Instant gratification has to be smashed from our everyday thinking. "Get me outta jail," "Can I have my paycheck early?" "I want to be rid of this disease now!" "I have to have (fill in your own item here) now." We've all said these statements at one time or another. Thinking that the world revolved around me was always a given. I was a deserving kind of guy. Doesn't everyone know how much I give back on a daily basis? Now it's my turn . . . GIMME! This is, in my opinion, the hardest of the four.

For 23 years of hard, active addiction, it was next to impossible to change patterns I knew so well. My alter ego fed off of this and eventually was smashed. I was left alone with this broken ego and had to learn how to rebuild my life—without getting what I wanted. I went to others for advice, therapists, meetings, counselors, and a sponsor to see what they did, and how they did it. The conclusion I came to was that I was afraid to be myself and worried too much what others thought of me. For acceptance, I could become whoever you wanted me to be. Sometimes, it was fun to pretend to be someone else, but the consequences were always the same and I always ended up being alone. This ability carried over into the recovery world because if I let people into my life and showed them the real me, they would make jokes behind my back and eventually embarrass me in front of others.

This brings me to the fourth: balance. Once I started to lead a spiritual existence and find my center point, I let God guide my life for me. As a result, I found love within myself and that enabled me to love others; even if they did talk behind my back, judge me, or embarrass me in front of others. I cannot control people or their actions. Most of the time, the fear was gone.

But I am human, and I am not made of stone or perfect in any way. I believe with a good balance, or center, that includes honesty, willingness, spiritual guidance, and being open-minded, one can finally grow and finally lay to rest most of their insecurities.

In some instances, a fear of the past lingers in our head and memories. For me, I call this "SEM" (Search Engine Marketing) because that's when I started using and began a life of loneliness and searching. I took my first drug when I was 13, and I literally stopped growing emotionally. And when I stopped using, my brain was still at the age of 13. I had many demons that SEM had to face. Time after time, I would recover until I had to finally look at my past, my demons, my mistakes, and my nightmares and face them. Every time I did, I shut down and basically excused myself from growing, which resulted in more drinking and more drugging. What does your inner self have hidden? Some things we hide we think no one will understand. We think we are unique, different. We are not. My alter ego SEM still lingers today.

There's a story I heard somewhere many years ago in a meeting. It's a story to remind us that no matter what you may have done, there is always someone out there who has done the same thing or something worse.

> There was a man who went into an AA meeting to finally get some help. He had had enough and wanted to get better. But he was ashamed of his past and decided to sit in the back of the room and just listen. He did this for a straight week and finally decided that if he wanted to get better, he had to let go of his darkest secrets. So, on the seventh day, he stood up at the end of the meeting, introduced himself as an alcoholic and stated he liked to have sex with chickens when he was drunk. The room went dead quiet. Finally, one guy in the front of the room spoke up and said, "Did your chicken die too?"

Whatever you are holding onto, let it go. Give it to God and let yourself grow. You deserve it.

What are my inner strengths? What makes me, me? As an alcoholic, I am so used to focusing on the negative behaviors or wreckage I have caused. For a long time, I thought I didn't have anything to offer to anyone. It wasn't until a family meeting, which was held through my counselor, that I discovered I had attributes that others saw in me. I found I had leadership qualities and potential, a great sense of humor; I am a loving and caring father and ex-husband, and I deeply care for other people. Can you find your own attributes? If you aren't able to have a counseling session like I did, ask your family, friends, sponsor, or even more simply, grab a piece of paper and list what you think your strengths might be. Be honest. God loves you and will guide you in your journey. If you are sincere, you will come up with at least three, and as your sobriety continues to grow, so will your list. Mine grows every 6 months, it seems.

Don't be afraid of yourself. Society itself is an oddity that judges you, and others, without knowing who we are inside. The sober society we live in contains over one million brothers and sisters worldwide and they will love us for who we are. Wherever we go, there we are. Be strong, be loved, and remember to love yourself. In time, you will know who you are, and I'll be willing to bet that if you work a solid program, you won't give one damn what others think of you—sober or not. You will discover that fear itself will dissolve away and be replaced with strength, courage, and the ability to open up and release your fears! "Fear is born from the Devil. It has no beginning or end. It is eternal, omnipotent!"[1]

The point of this quote is to show that no matter what, fear will always be a factor in some way. Think back to when we were children. What was it that you were afraid of? I was afraid of my dad, the dark, and vampires. Even as a child, I knew I had to find a solution. With the dark and vampire thing, I simply hid under my covers with a flashlight. As for my pops, I hid in my closet or behind the garage in the backyard.

Now speed up the clock until our addictions were at their worse . . . what were we afraid of then? All of us ran away from one thing or another in order to "hide" from our demon, or "vampire." Some of us hid in a bottle, some in a rig, some in a little baggie, in church, in work, in a bad relationship, and so on. The list can go on.

We had to face life head-on if we were to have any chance to recover. For such a long time, our demon prevented us from smashing the insecurities and letting go of our fear. We looked to others for a solution. We found safety in meetings, sponsors, or the company of another drunk or addict. At our meetings, we were able to release our garbage, and as a result, it took away the power of fear. Sometimes we will feel "less than" if we open up to someone or speak out in a meeting. This is not true! If anything, it will make us stronger. My pops used to say an old German concept that went: "What does not kill us, will only make us stronger!"[2] Of course, he would literally say it in German.

Realization shows that fears are inevitable. But we also need to know that there are healthy fears in the program that can help and guide us to stay sane and sober. In a residential treatment setting, men and women who have done 28 days or more graduate back into society with, and sometimes without, a treatment plan. Look at their eyes. The ones who have no fear or concern in them usually are drunk within 24 to 72 hours upon their release. The addict who is discharged with the "look" or "stare" is more likely to stay on track and maintain sobriety. These people have just enough fear in them to do whatever is necessary to stay sober. These are the ones who remember what is waiting for them—jails, psycho wards, and funerals. Work the twelve steps and fear and insecurity will disappear. People will pound a lot of knowledge and the Big Book down your throat. Take what you need and leave the rest. Trust me on this. There is this semi-old-timer where I lived in Austin, Texas who preached the word of AA. Everyone looked up to him, including me. I was so lost in my addiction that if anyone with half a mind told me that if I ate airplane glue daily, it would keep me sober, I'd do it.

This old man preached and preached and I followed. He became my sponsor and I even lived in his home. He talked a mean program, but when it came to actually living it himself, he fell way short. At home, he whined about bullshit and at meetings he would say that the little things don't sweat him anymore. I knew the real drunk a lot of others didn't. So guys and gals, always remember that it is your recovery and you can choose whatever piece of information helps you to stay sober. There is more than one way.

Confront your fears. Let others confront you without any judgment cast back on them. This process helps us take a look inside and deal with the challenges at hand. This process will reveal itself in the step work. I worked steps one through twelve trying to find the answers to my problems. Turns out the problem was me. And the funny thing was that I ended up relieving myself of most fears without even knowing it. God took care of it for me. All I had to do was buck up, suit up, and show up. Everything I worried about was pretty much gone by the eleventh step. Once I was willing to confront my own shit and acknowledge my own fears, then they had no power. My peers also pointed out fears in me that caused me to work twice as hard. Again, they disappeared and I was left with euphoria and a new way of thinking. I've seen brothers and sisters in AA accomplish the same, and they are much happier. But then there are those, like myself in the past, that would not deal with or confront their fears; relapse was there always keeping them from getting better. In my research from 1994, I interviewed four homeless crack addicts and alcoholics. After listening to their stories and asking the standardized questions, all four of them said that in one way or another, fear of the past would come back to them in the future.

They felt calmer and more secure running and hustling the streets at night. Why did they choose that way of life and yet continue to stay in this life choice? One must wonder what kind of past emotional garbage existed that was so bad that they preferred the street and drug life over any chance of help or sobriety.

After we reach a point in our own recovery, it is vital that we reach out and offer help to other drunks and addicts like ourselves. I wish I could have helped those gentlemen I interviewed, but they were not ready or willing to receive any type of help—from me or anyone. I have to respect that. You just can't help someone if they are not ready or willing. If and when you get hooked into a home group, eventually you will see someone come through the doors, either for their first time in AA or rebounding off of a relapse. They will be afraid and broken, and it will be up to you to reach out and make them feel welcome. Be sure to be patient, tolerant, and understanding. And make sure your actions are pure. There will always be that guy out there willing to reach out to the newcomer female and want to "save" her. In reality, they are only looking for sex, and known in our community as "thirteen steppers." So ladies, if you are sober and want to help, keep these idiotic men away from these girls. It's up to you to step up and help the new girl coming in from the street.

And guys, do the right thing and help the new guy. Everybody can help each other so that no one has to walk alone. Just do the right thing.

The next chapter is designed for those who may have gone through a similar situation like I will be describing.

CHAPTER 2
CRAZY DOES IT

> "If you want to know what it is like to be hit
> on the head with a hammer, ask another nail!"

What you are about to read is a real and documented 5-day journal of my personal notes while I was in a psychiatric hospital in Austin, Texas, for suicidal thoughts and behaviors.

I felt that adding this was a necessary means to understanding what a person with a dual diagnosis goes through. It is not a war story. These events I am sharing are what I and many others face, see, and deal with almost on a daily basis. If any of this sounds like you, firstly, you are never alone. And secondly, you should seek immediate attention and get help so you may recover fully.

Six months before the psych ward, I was diagnosed with kidney cancer and any happy feelings or thoughts I may have had went down the drain. All I could do was to sit on the couch, in pain and be depressed. Not only that, my head was filled with death and thoughts of suicide. The only person I could think of leaving behind if I passed away was my daughter. So sadness and a mild form of insanity began to take control and grow within me. At this time, the only people I had told about the cancer and its pain were my parents, my boss, my roommate, and my ex-wife. Everyone else can wait, and enjoy the holidays without worrying about me and my health.

As time went by, I had the surgery to remove the cancer, and began the therapy to be able to manage the pain so I could get back to work. This was harder than I thought. First off, the fear that I believed they didn't get all the cancer was always buzzing in my head. Then, there was the fact that standing and walking for long periods of time was causing tremendous amounts of pain. And the worst... the worst part was all the physical and psychological trauma my body and I went through post-surgery. But it didn't stop there, because I checked into a psych ward. Here is my story:

Day 1

It is March of '09 and the doctors are saying I am having a bipolar episode. It's going horribly wrong. Dr. "L" has been over-medicating me for 4 days. I spent the entire time knocked out in bed. On the fourth day, he discharged me for being "untreatable." Shortly thereafter, I fell into a massive state of depression. I stayed there till I obtained my fourth DWI, which was later dropped. At this point, I wanted to kill myself. And I was serious. If I had been alone and had the means to do so, I would have made the attempt. But I didn't. When I got out of jail, I lost my job, and got lost in the system. I now see a multitude of counselors, attend an outpatient group, and have an intoxalock system attached to my car.

Throughout all of this, I have had a lot of support from my father and friends in AA. I would love to list them all, but because of the anonymity of the program, I cannot. Everyone has been encouraging, but because I am self-loathing and have a lot of fear, I stay stuck in a hole I cannot seem to crawl out of. But I talk. I talk to those that will listen. I talk to those that can relate. The inner demons and voices continually tell me I am worthless. They tell me I will never make it anywhere or accomplish anything in my life. They tell me I will never find true love with anyone. My goal is to fail. My objective is to be the outcast, the loser I was destined to be. The only safe place for me is within these psychiatric walls—confined and medicated so I do not rage out to anyone. And believe me when I say that I will if given the chance! Or will I?

Day 2

The day has now come to an end, and everyone is medicated in one form or another. Most are asleep, but I'm still going. Even after using my meds and adding some on top of them, I continue to think and write and remain insane. When people think of insanity, they assume the worst. They immediately think of the guy who talks to and answers himself. They think of the girl with the ragged look, crying uncontrollably in her room for hours on end. And mostly, they think of the guy who is angry and wants to fight, or rages that if given the chance he would shoot up the place, killing a handful of people and then turning the gun on himself. If you think that there are people here like that, you're right. Wherever we go, there we are. But then, there is also the type who by all appearances is sane. Their vision is focused, their thoughts are sharp and controlled, and they have the ability to adapt to whatever environment they are dropped into. Think about that. Is there someone in your life that you think you know like this?

I look around the floor that has been locked down tight. I see nurses and orderlies: heavy ones, pretty ones, average ones, butch ones, and male ones. They always scamper around doing their job. And most of them are doing it with a smile. Why is it they smile? Is it because they take pride in their job? Are they happy to be employed with the recession going on? Or is it because they have access to the best psychiatric meds insurance money can buy? It's hard to be smiling that much with twenty plus mentally unstable patients running around. I mean, we're the lunatics! I have taken a rather large cocktail of medications which should have knocked me out flat on the floor. It will just be a matter of time before they offer me an even stronger cocktail to take.

Although being locked down inside of this psych ward does make me feel safe, the sadness, depression, and loneliness has intensified. My brain is in overdrive, and my thoughts race from my first drink of booze at the age of 13 all the way to my fourth pending DWI. I think about all the stupid mistakes I have made; I ate out of dumpsters, begged for change for that next drink, hurt my family and friends, and made legal trouble for myself with the lies. Most of the time, I deal with it. But there are "black days" where it is just too much to handle. That's when I blow up internally and the fear takes over. Here in treatment, the guardians/nurses and staff walk right by you and pay no mind to you and what you are doing. But then again, a slump of a face, a blank stare or constant drooling doesn't qualify as a need for assistance. And when the fear starts to happen enough, I suddenly start to boil, and the choice to let it out is now questionable. Now they will start to notice! My idol, Homer J.

Simpson, once said something along these lines about anger: "Take all your anger and stuff it down in a place deep inside of you. And one day when it is too much, it'll just come out all at once . . . remember when daddy threw the whiskey bottle at that umpire? Hmm? Yea . . . you do."[1]

Day 3

The problem I had in junior high school is pretty much the same problem(s) I have today. I remember in eighth grade, I was outside after lunch with about a hundred kids. Even though they were all around me, interacting with me and each other, I still felt all alone and isolated. And one day, as this same thing was happening, I had my first thought of killing myself. And as the thought came into my head as clear as day, I threw up. Now here I am as an adult feeling the same way, with all the stomach problems I can handle. Let me make one thing clear people: I am not constantly in a psych ward, and I am not constantly wanting to hurt myself. As I have explained in the beginning of these writings, I have gone through a lot in the last six months! Tomorrow I may want to kiss the sky. Or the day after that I may want to suck on the end of a shotgun . . . who knows?

While within these psychiatric walls, a voice deep inside keeps telling me to push ahead; I am not alone. That voice, that sweet wonderful voice, is the voice of my pops. Since this whole disease started and began to take control of my mind and body, my pops has dedicated himself to being the best cheerleader and coach a guy like me could ever ask for. He has educated himself on the study of alcoholism and depression as well as my mom has. She is a black belt Al-Anon. Sometimes, she gets stuck in one way of thinking and will not budge. I love her, but I think she could learn to see both sides to a cup. My pops had a history in his family of the disease, so obviously he wouldn't want either of his sons to go through the things his family went through. It is too bad that it took AA and the whole process within itself to bring us closer together. Pops would tell me he is my biggest fan, in the closest bleachers—if you will—cheering me on. And he does. My pops is not the type to show his emotions to anyone, but when I pay enough attention, I catch a few of them that he lets get by. We both have a hard time telling each other how we feel when we are face-to-face, but

I'll email him with thoughts and feelings sometimes just to let him know how much I love him.

Day 4

When I checked into this hellhole of a hospital 4 days ago, I went through the initial intake process of admittance. First, all the basics were taken: blood, urine, weight, and pulse. Then the questions start . . . it's always the goddamn questions. They wanted to know my name, my address, if I've ever been in a treatment facility or psych hospital, and if I've ever thought of hurting myself. As for the facilities, I answered yes but never admitted to how many. Thirteen, to be precise. And psych wards? Five.

Now onto the hurting myself thing. Their question was a little broad. It could mean a suicide attempt, getting into fights I knew I was going to lose, putting my hands and head through walls, taking way too many medications, and/or romancing the thought of inflicting pain upon myself. That last one has been constantly running throughout my stay here. I know what they do to you when you admit to any of those. So I looked them in the eye, smiled, and said, "No. No thoughts like that ma'am." If only they knew the truth.

Well, it's a new day. Some of the crazies are already arguing about nothing. Once again, the techs and nurses are just smiling. I've been medicated so far with a nicotine patch, Tylenol, and at 9:00 a.m. I get my anxiety meds. I hope they work. Last night, they doubled my Seroquel to 300 mg, gave me something for anxiety and an Ambien. Three hours later, they gave me another Ambien. Still nothing! I ended up talking to the walls. Then a nurse ended up giving me a Benadryl shot which finally worked and knocked me on my ass. I dreamt of my daughter, cartoons, and happy things for the next 6 hours. Then I woke up. Stupid reality. And all the pain, depression, and sadness came right back, as if it was clockwork. But, like my pops used to say, no matter how bad you may feel, there is always someone worse off than you are. So I sit and observe. It's like watching a bunch of primates solve a scenario to get a banana down from the ceiling which was hanging by a cord. The addicts and the insane gather together, and when asked to come to a solution, it is like they are throwing feces at each other hoping that the other side will give up and eventually convert to the other side. This is better than TV.

My mental history goes back as far as I can remember. There were a lot of outbursts when I was younger. I'd punch holes in the walls, punch my brother and his friends, yell at my parents and teachers, and my mind was always racing with thoughts. Amazingly, I never had a hospitalization until I was 28. That particular establishment was rough and disturbing. I manipulated their program so they could get just enough of what they wanted. So when I left, I was the same way as when I'd entered—mental.

Day 5

Here's an interesting tidbit and entry to this chapter. As I write, my blood pressure is rising, my heart feels like it is going to explode, and any means of calmness within me is now gone and being replaced with the rage which is completely taking over. I want to tear apart the dining room. It's only a matter of time before my inner demon finds a way out and does what he does best. It's not pretty, and the last thing I want is to be put in restraints. Please God, help me. Whenever I get pushed over the edge or way too drunk, "he" comes out. "He" makes the worst decisions. When I'm piss drunk, I know I am responsible. But still, there is a part of me that is completely not me.

Right now, the psychotic part is boiling. I look around the room and see nothing but weak people. People I could easily crush or harm without a second thought. God, if I don't get out of this safe, it looks like you are gonna have to deal with me! I hate feeling like this. This state of mind takes me back to high school. More specifically, military school. I was fine and functioned well until my senior year when one evening, I got into a fight. He was on top of me, pounding my kidneys, and all I could do was laugh while he hit me over and over. Then I tasted blood and wiped my lip. It was dark red. My frame of mind changed almost instantly. I beat the living hell outta him and kicked him in the face until he passed out. Even then, I had to have two guys pull me off of him. He had to spend two days in the sick bay. I vowed to never fight again.

But the suppressed rage waits. And when I least suspect it—bam! It comes out in the form of yelling, shaking, crying, or self-destruction. But not fighting. But now, years later, I am able to recognize the warning signs and deal with it semi-appropriately. The only problem was that 1) it took forever to control, and 2) the doctors never put the right meds in me when I needed them. I had to rely on my everyday medications. By the grace of God, somehow they worked. I am slowly getting back to normal. The techs do not have a clue how lucky they were tonight. I'm sure they would have taken me down, but one or two would have gone down with me!

On a lighter note, I feel like I'm on a vacation from my problems, and society in general. This hospital is far from a resort, but it isn't county jail either. It lies somewhere in the middle.

Remember the movie *What about Bob?* with Bill Murray and Richard Dreyfuss? When Dr. Marvin—Dreyfuss—tells Bob—Bill Murray—to take a vacation from his problems, Bob appears to become a new man. So I am deciding to do the same thing: a vacation from myself and the challenges that await me in the outside world. I know that when I am discharged in 40 hours, all the challenges will be waiting for me. Those of you out there with the same crippling emotional problems I have; would you be willing to face your challenges if you knew you had a countdown of 40 hours to be released back into society? This week has been both restful and stressful. But I am hoping the proper doses of medications are in order. This hospital is not the best, and I only think of how much they can charge you for this or that, but it'll have to do. If only they had back-up meds for rageaholics and other violent people, then people like me, and worse, could have immediate help and therapy.

I think back in my life and see my anger, greed, sloth, manipulation, and the choices I made with and without my parents' guidance. Either way, here I am, by my own means, in a psychiatric environment. Once again, wherever I go, there I am.

5 hours till discharge

As I get ready to leave, I am scared and nervous about walking out those doors. But on the other side of the coin, I feel a little levelheaded and not so miserable. So there may be another chance at life for me beyond these walls. And so, the journey begins. Peace out!

The National Alliance on Mental Illness, or NAMI, have listed some major mental illnesses. I am not going to define them for you since that would not help me help you. Look them up yourself, you lazy bastard! But they list eight. They are: Schizophrenia, Bipolar Disorder (1 and 2), Major Depression, Borderline Personality Disorder, Anxiety Disorders, Panic Disorder, OCD, and PTSD. Thank God for Google, eh?

If given a proper diagnosis by a professional doctor, there are components of recovery which could guide you and keep you on a path that just may be tolerable. The components of recovery are: Dark Days, Acceptance, Treatment, Coping Strategies, Success, Hopes, and Dreams. Most groups and organizations I personally do not believe in. But NAMI is the exception to my ideals. For more information on them, drop them a line at info@nami.org. Now enough free publicity for them. Back to the chapter before my meds wear off.

My family raised me as well as they could. They were involved in my sports, school, work, and family vacation getaways. I have talked about my father, but now let me tell you about my mother. She is a beautiful, strong and loving person.

Growing up, she was the one who was there when I was sick, when my young heart was broken, when I scraped a knee, and when it was time to discipline. When the addiction began, she tried so very hard to be supportive and loving. But I made it almost impossible for her to do so. As a result, she entered Al-Anon and learned to live life for herself. Sure, part of me wishes we were that mother-son team we used to be. But I watch her, and see how far she has come. I am ever so proud of her. The only challenge is that we are not as close as we used to be. I will miss that. I love my mother, a.k.a. Pepe, and will always try to be the son she wants.

Somewhere along the span of my life, I was bored and needed an adventure. I found it, but I think the devil actually found me. The scene was nothing like I had ever imagined it to be . . . the music, the nightlife, the women, and let's not forget the DRUGS! We will come back to discuss my favorite sin in detail later.

But up to this point, this is the life I chose for 20 years. It would seem God does not want me in His kingdom above because He knows I would end up trashing the place. But, why would He take some of my closest friends who had done a lot less than I did? It's not right. But these friends will never be forgotten. Ever!

Anyways, to wrap up this psychobabble chapter on an inside look into my mind and frame of it—I believe doing this will help people understand that even though they may think they are the only ones who go through stuff like this, they are not. We are all in the same boat at one point or another.

As for my rage and fighting, I can honestly say that I have not been in a fight since that day in 1991, and I have learned through therapy and groups to work on my rage. But that little demon still sits and waits for me to get really mad. Then he does what he likes to do best. It's like having the "Hulk" living inside of me.

Except I don't hitchhike everywhere I go and have piano music playing softly as I do it.

As you will notice, this book and its contents may jump around from spirituality, to my story, to challenges, or to "as it happens" writing. This alone explains why it has taken so long for this to get onto the shelves and into your hands. How many of you out there have felt like me, gone through the same situations like me, or even worse? Don't answer that quite yet. Finish the book and then let me know.

CHAPTER 3
THE STORY

I was born on September 8, 1972, in Houston, Texas, at St. Joseph's hospital. I was a bastard child to a single mother who was the daughter of a Baptist minister. She wanted the best for me, and decided adoption was the best answer. I was quickly adopted by my parents and raised in a loving and caring home. My childhood was as normal and fun as any other child in the neighborhood. My parents gave birth to my brother two years after my adoption. My brother, Patrick, and I had a pretty normal sibling rivalry until we discovered how to argue and fight. This went on well into junior high. Anyway, as a child, I had a remarkable imagination and a sense of creativity. My parents nourished this seed in hopes it would grow into something beautiful. And it did . . . for the most part.

In fifth grade, my thinking and learning process started to take a turn, and eventually came to a dead stop. If an assignment was given in class, I did okay. But if it was something to take home and study for a test the following day, I just could not retain the information until the next day at test time. Therefore, three-quarters of all my exams from fifth grade onward were either failing grades or "skin of my teeth" passing ones. I didn't recognize then, as I do now, how upset this made me. I thought it was normal what I getting. So, to cover and divert this feeling, I became a class clown. Obviously, I made a lot of friends and got a lot of attention.

I need to back up a bit and explain some emotional garbage that ties into this equation. I had a secret. From the time I was born until the ripe age of 16, I was a chronic bedwetter. Something medical and/or psychological was causing this. And as a child, there were times I was asked to sleep over at

The Story

a friend's house. Talk about embarrassing! Without going into detail, you'd be amazed by how many times I was able to hide what I did and also not hide what I did. Once it made my mom so mad that she actually hit me with either her hand, a belt, or a cord of some type. I don't remember the details, as I seem to have blocked out most of it.

Now, skip ahead to junior high, and I'm scared out of my mind. In my observations and experiences, this is when kids start to form and develop cliques to hang and socialize in. Everyone reading this knows what I am talking about, so there is no need to define them. The point of the matter is the fact that the friends I used to have dispersed into smaller, more organized groups, and everyone made fun of each other's cliques. Some kids had started smoking, while others were athletic, and others still were skaters . . . and so on, and so on. Where did I fit in? Nowhere. I felt like the kid who was always picked last at sports. I just kept to myself with my head down, and tried my best to get along with everyone. I also discovered two things I never noticed before. One was the opposite sex, and the other was a "terminal" stomach issue I still fight with to this day. My mom used to volunteer in the junior high's infirmary. She worked with the school nurse, who, by the way, is a wonderful woman who cared for over 50,000 children before she retired, and I would go in pretty much every day complaining of stomach pains and cramps. They thought it was cute because they believed I was only there to see my mom. Granted, it was nice to see her, but it wasn't her I was there to see.

Girls . . . wow. Someone had pulled the blindfold away from my eyes and a whole new outlook had opened up for me. I liked their smell, their smiles, and their batting eyes when they wanted me to carry their backpacks for them. But the problem was that I was too damn afraid to talk to any of them. Period! I would go out of my way to avoid a girl if I even remotely thought she was cute. I even acted like a buffoon and assumed they thought it was cute. I had neither self-esteem nor confidence. I could never express my feelings on how I felt toward anyone in particular, so I would latch onto the type of girl that had the same type of problems I was having. And if I could find one that was worse than me . . . Watch out, mamma.

Then, one day, they noticed me. I don't know why or how, but they did. As a result, I got my first girlfriend. Let's call her Jennifer. Being with

Jennifer was great. She had a sense of humor and a personality I could wrap myself into. She later became my "first." Anyways, while I was with her, the first sign of my addiction began to surface. In our world, this meant one was great, but more was better. Not more of Jennifer, but more intimacy with as many girls as I could get. So I began my search. I fooled around with as many girls as I could handle. At one time, I was juggling six girls at once. I was big into kissing and heavy petting. It got to the point that Jennifer could tell by my style of kissing that I was with someone else besides her. Guys, girls have their own style when they are with that one person with whom they love and want to be with. I broke that poor girl's heart on more than one occasion. I have no idea why she stuck it out with me for as long as she did.

Another thing happened that same year. I discovered alcohol. I was over at a friend's house for a sleepover in which we planned to stay up all night and play Dungeons & Dragons. Another friend of mine at the same sleepover, let's call him blockhead, had brought over a half-full bottle of Johnny Walker scotch. No one knew how to properly drink this foul-smelling liquid. So, like you see in so many movies, I grabbed the bottle from him, put it to my lips, and tipped the bottle straight up. Now, you drunks out there think I let that sweet nectar of the gods run down my throat and into my belly giving me that oh-so-good feeling, right? Wrong, my friends! Maybe an ounce hit the back of my throat causing a burning sensation and an instant gag effect. Vomit sprayed the room like a sprinkler watering a yard. I didn't pick up another drink for 3 more years.

Junior high came and went, and what replaced that? High school. Now I was even more scared. By now, a fifth of my friends had become stoners or burnouts. Others had become skaters, while others had become goth. The last ones were jocks, snobs, and leftovers. And that's what I settled for—a leftover. My attention and grades had gotten so bad that I no longer cared. So now I became angry. Not at anyone in particular, but it was the type of anger that an addict stuffs deep down inside.

Halfway through my freshman year, I was given the opportunity to attend a school called the Marine Military Academy. My father is a Marine, so I thought this would make him proud. I packed my bags with high hopes and a new motivation to become something in life. At the airport, there were other cadets going back from Christmas break. It seemed they walked a little taller and had more pride than say the average joe walking around in this airport. I wanted that. It was time to board the plane and I hugged my mom, who cried, shook my brother's hand, and went to hug my dad. My father pulled me into his arms, hard, then pushed me away while he cried. He just walked away. What in God's name was I getting myself into?

There is no real need to go into great detail about life at the Marine Military Academy. Or as we called it on the inside, the Marine mental asylum. The school itself changed a lot of young men. Scholastically, my grades sucked which meant a lot of summer school. My superior officers beat me the hell up, pushed me to my physical limits, and degraded me to the fullest extent.

But the brainwashing kept me coming back for more. I transformed into a mean, null, void, and dangerous person. I hated it, but my psyche loved it!

The real and main reason I wanted to write about the academy, was the alcoholism. This monument is the source of my chaos. Every cadet's pastime on the weekend was to get as drunk, high, or blacked out as you could. And many of us tried as hard as we could. I was finally accepted! I was somebody around these men.

I was a man. I had also made a close friend. We'll call him "Jaybo." With him, there was such a variety of cocktails of narcotics, booze, and clubs. He once turned me on to a little pill called ecstasy. I instantly fell in love with this drug. It didn't give off a booze-like smell, I was always aware of my surrounding, I didn't slur my words, and I always remembered the night before. Don't get me wrong, when there was no X around, I drank like a goddamn fish. But for the next five years, X would be my master for the most part.

When quarterly and summer vacations came around, Jaybo and I lived and drank in two specific bars (by the way, thanks to Bill and Erick for the memories). Since at the time we were underage, the names of these two bars will stay a secret. But being as it was, it became a ritual. In the four years and four summers together, there were probably a total of ten days where he and I didn't hang out and get really drunk. Whatever I did, he did. Whatever he did, I did. He was my best friend in the world. When we hit our senior year, I was given the keys to the cadet club. This was a dance hall and snack bar for the cadets. But there was a DJ booth. And that became the beginning of the end for me. I had no idea that being a DJ would almost kill me.

My alcohol and drug use was at an all-time high during this phase in my life. I was still able to have a good time, and suffed very little consequences. This is what I refer as the innocent era. My first summer after high school graduation, I landed my first DJ career job. It wasn't much, but it did help my ego inflate a little more. My stage name was DJ Weasel B. This was also about the time I used cocaine for the first time. It was beyond amazing! But when my friend flipped me again and showed how to combine X and cocaine, the angels above sung and the Earth moved. Now my innocent era was fizzling out and being replaced with pure self-destruction. I no longer cared about anything. Women came and went without a second thought about what their names were. I took what I needed and then kicked them to the curb. But I was so good at this, I could make it to where they would throw themselves out. My lies became more and more frequent. My personal outlook on life was nothing but gloom. I honestly believed how I was living and the beliefs I had were completely normal. This is how people lived. My addiction had just hit a whole new low.

I went to college in Henniker, New Hampshire, during the fall of 1991. Once again, I was new and unknown to anyone. And being from the Deep South, cultures collided. It was a living and breathing acid trip with the legs of a lizard and the eyes of a statue. So I started drinking as quickly as I could find a source. In doing so, I quickly adapted to my new environment and eased myself into groups I felt comfortable. But I did still have structure and military thinking process. I still jogged 3 miles a day, cleaned my room daily, and made sure to get to class. This wonderful structure did not last long once I realized there was no one to hold me accountable. Within a month, I was a grungy slob, heavy smoker, and an advocate for the use of weed. I also started drinking a lot more than I should have been. It appeared as if I was trying to do 18 years of drinking in a very little amount of time. I only lasted a semester in college before, wouldn't you know it, I had my first run in with the law. There was an assault charge brought up against me that was completely bogus. But in the beginning of this whole ordeal, not a single person believed me and my innocence. I was judged before I was found guilty or innocent of anything. The local police kept me awake and questioned me for 14 hours. All this time, I was drunk and scared. After this long and cruel punishment of a flimsy legal system, I went to jail in Concord, New Hampshire. I became reclusive, fearful, sad, guilty, and full of rage.

So, what happens next, you might wonder? I was released on bond to my parents, and after the final say so toward my conditions on where I would be living, I returned to Houston to live with my parents... So now I had to find a way to escape from my insanity. I found the first thing that came around—cocaine and scotch. My mind was a sack of rotten monkey crap, and I didn't care. I decided to stay in this funk till either the court shit was over or I was dead. And I tried to die, believe that! The bottom line is this: from 1992 to 1999, my cocaine habit was $1,300 a week and I was drinking 1.5 liters of scotch a day. I was always broke. I cried myself to sleep every night that I didn't pass out from being drunk, and constantly fought off nose bleeds from snorting a shit load of coke. And I weighed in at 120 lbs.

I remember thinking during the few times I was sober that I really did wish I was dead. Not by sucking on the end of a colt .45 long slide pistol or cutting my wrists with a 10" Ka-Bar. But by means of an overdose, drunk driver, robbery gone bad, or something cool like that. I eventually sunk into a depression I can only describe as "the black period." But in my mind, as long as I had drugs, the pain would stay away and I wouldn't have to face it. So like everything else in life to better my integrity, I started smoking crack. Good choice, right? This fun addiction started in the mid-1990s. And it had its hold on me.

My folks didn't know what to do or what to think. Being non-emotional at the time, they did what they knew to do: "Speak no evil, hear no evil." And the blinders came on. Once, they did try to give me a small intervention in 1990. They found some of my X I had hidden in my room for later use. When they tried to talk to me and let me know what I was doing to them, I shut down and my conman came out. He said everything they wanted to hear, and then some. The man even threw in some tears to seal the deal. It worked, and I'd evaded rehab . . . so far.

So jump to 1993. To be more specific, August 13, 1993. This was the day my rebirth began. I just didn't know it at the time. My parents and my brother were out at a soccer game and I was home alone inhaling god-awful amounts of cocaine. I knew they would be home soon and I had a bright idea, on coke, to evade my family as they came home. I would scale across the roof and climb down a fence to make my getaway. Did that ever backfire on me! Once I got to the edge of the roof, I slipped, fell, and broke my right leg clean in half—all this in a matter of minutes.

Before my body and mind could register there was about to be a tremendous amount of pain, I took my wallet that was full of cocaine and buried it next to the fence. As the pain started to run through my body, I crawled away from the burial site and started to scream uncontrollably at the top of my lungs. My mom, dad, and brother were driving up at this point, and they somehow heard me. Not only that, but I woke the neighbors nine houses away and everyone in between. Haven't talked to anyone on my parents' street since that day.

An ambulance pulled up and procedure states that they take vitals for information to relay to the doctors. They, of course, saw my elevated blood pressure, increased heart rate, and let's not forget the sweat dripping down my face. The tech flat-out asked if I was on any speed or narcotic at that very moment in time. I lied. If my parents knew, they would disown me. He asked again, and again I lied. He then went on to tell me that I would not be able to receive a painkiller shot till he knew what was in my system. Mmmmmm . . . painkillers. No matter how it happened in the beginning, I had to tell the truth in order to get help. I openly admitted my cocaine addiction to someone. And so, a new chapter opened in my life. Meeting my best friend was coming around the corner and I had no idea.

The EMT disappeared from the back of the ambulance. I'm almost positive he went and told my parents. After an agonizing wait, they finally closed the doors, and off to the hospital I went.

Once I got to the hospital, the waiting around was horrible. I wasn't a priority. Once my blood pressure and heart rate went back down to almost normal, I was able to get pain relief. After several hours, I was wheeled into the ER and they began to work on my leg. God I love that stuff they use to knock you out!

I woke up in recovery with a fog I'd never felt before. My leg was in a cast from toes to hip. Now, up to this exact point in my life, I never believed in angels and that they watched over people. I believed in God through the church, but never angels. I now believe He sent just that, an angel to give me a message. As I had said, the room was dark, but at the corner edge of my bed sat a woman in white clothing looking very calm and serene. The first thing she said was that I didn't have to live like a sinner. She meant dope fiend I'm sure. She also said that many, many, many good things were to come my way. Like I said, I was bitter, mean, and close minded. I wasn't wanting to hear what she had to say. I couldn't "listen to the message." But I was also confined to a bed, so I was stuck there. She never asked me to speak or respond. She talked about life, God, and choices. This took about 10 minutes from beginning to end. Then she was gone. The morphine slowly started to make its way inside my brain and unleash a euphoria like no other. Morphine's great, but you gotta be broken to get some. Totally worth it. I dreamt of angels.

I awoke the next day to my parents leering over me—looking, waiting, observing. The pain was horrible. My mom told me much later that the only words to cross my lips before I passed back out was, "I have never felt pain like this in my entire life!" Three days and a lot of morphine later, I was sent home. My doctor's hope was that the cast would heal my leg on its own. I was confined to the couch. It was so boring. So I did what any self-respecting addict would do. I went and dug up my coke, laid out a couple of lines, and got really high.

Not only that, I had my dealer bring me more while my parents were in the house at the time, already concerned about the whole situation. So for the next 3 days, I lay on the couch and snorted hoards of cocaine. Do you realize how hard it is to keep quiet the sound of snorting and sniffing at three o'clock in the morning? It ain't easy.

We went back to the doctor's office and had a couple of x-rays done. The leg did not set. He said I had to go back under and have them operate on my legs—inserting an 8 mm and 12 inch steel rod through the bone of my tibia. So, once again, they put me on the slab and hooked up the IV. Here comes the colors...

I woke up feeling like Greggory Hines had tap danced all over my head. It hurt. It hurt bad. I don't recommend this to anyone. I spent 4 days in the hospital and used crutches to learn how to walk again. Really sucks. I was released with a big ol' medical boot on my right foot.

Back at my parents' house, I laid up on the couch another night. I resumed my hobby of shoving large amounts of coke up my nose. By morning, my nose was a bloody mess and I could not stop shaking from withdrawals. My mom stood over me and said that if I didn't get help, I had to leave. Shit! I'm a fucking cripple on the couch. What do I do? I agree. And for now, I had a roof over my head. I had no intention to get sober whatsoever. She then went on to tell me that a guy in recovery who was a counselor was coming over to talk to me. Again, shit!

A little old beat-up car pulled up in front of my parents' house. What stepped out was my answer, my cure. I didn't see that at the time. What I saw was a Gallagher look-alike. I was looking for his mallet. I adapted quickly; I improvised and overcame the situation to my favor. Not. He saw through me. His name was Pat. And now, 17 years later, my best friend. He stood on his soap box and talked about drugs and recovery. It was a cult. His speech went in one ear and right out the other. At the end of his rant, I blindly agreed to attend his outpatient group. I would ride it through and lie till something better came along and presented itself. One week later, I was sitting in a room with six other "addicts." Every one of them was younger than me. There's no reason to tell you what went on in that group. Just feast your eyes on this one little excerpt from the first week of therapy. I was about to turn 21 in about 3 days. The leader asked me what I was going to do for this special day. I said I was going to go get blind, stinking drunk and throw up somewhere I will not remember in the morning. He did not like that answer. He started quoting the "Big Book," which I thought was some cult membership reading. Every one of the AA people I met kept talking "Big Book" this and "Big Book" that. I didn't care. He asked the room what they thought about my decision to go out on my birthday. Everyone amazingly was on my side. So another session ends, and I feel I won this round. I stopped off at the corner store, like I always did after outpatient, and bought two beers for the road. As for my birthday, it went extremely well. A handful of painkillers and about five scotch and cokes can really make a party turn into a psychedelic amusement park. Living this lifestyle finally caught up with me. Within 2 years, I'd won two weekend getaways at two different times by driving while intoxicated on two occasions.

Oh yea, I'm lucky.

So for years, this was the way I lived, and one day it finally started to click. The things they were saying in the meetings started to make sense, and when I hung around these people, I did not use drugs or get thrown in jail. If only they could bottle that shit up and sell it; we would all be cured.

According to the laws of average, at this point in my life I should have been thrown in jail and forgotten about a long time ago. But alas, I walk a free man. You see, unfortunately there are people out there that for some strange reason love us. And for me, it was my parents. I did have loving and caring parents that wanted everything for me. But they were also very enabling to me. This was not their fault, we all are enabling to someone in our lives. I just know how to milk the feelings and issues related to my parents. Remember . . . addict! Ha! They would bail me out of jail every time, and I had good lawyers . . . for the most part of my life. But because of this, I constantly lied to everyone and I was completely uncreditable with everyone I knew. When I went to my meetings, I felt like there was no one here on the same drinking and drugging level that I was. And the people I hung out with were like me, but at the same time they were not like me at all. I seemed to use more, drink more, "party" more, and get in trouble more than any one of them. I had a never-grow-up attitude. All life was to me was one big, massive blackout party. When I trashed a friendship—either male or female, I would move on to another one until my self-centeredness and alcoholism would decay that one too. Finally, no one wanted to hang with me. I was alone. So many times, I locked myself in my apartment or bedroom to drink and smoke crack alone. Do you remember that feeling? I was a human waste disposal for a large number of chemicals. Some unknown to this day. Back then, I didn't care what I was doing to my body or how it would affect me in the future.

Well... here's future Wesley, to give you an update on exactly what happened. Other than the broken leg, there have been three open surgeries on my lower stomach, which my ex-wife so humorously calls the international border. One scar, as a matter of fact, was life threating surgery. Ah, good times. There was a battle with cancer which left a 9-inch scar across my right side. There was an ankle and a split in the back of my head hospital visits that ended with either a cast or stiches and a golf ball size knot on my head. Both of my knees are about 50% shot. My right shoulder I actually hurt in treatment recovering from drugs. HAHA HAHAHA!!! Talk about karma. The treatment center in Austin, Texas, refused to pay for medical assistance on more than one occasion.

Be careful to not get hurt in recovery in Austin. They're dicks with their money. But they sure know how to save a life. Oh, and a hernia in which they had to reopen my cancer scar to get to. Nice, eh? I move like an old man sometimes. But all of these are a direct consequence of my lifestyle and drug abuse. So if you are thinking it won't happen to you and I was a fluke accident, guess again. "*Sum Quad Eris!*" That means, "I am what you will be." You can thank my father for expanding your knowledge a little today. Seriously, thank him. Annoy the shit outta him with thank you cards. He taught me a little bit from a lot. He helps so many people for so many reasons, and never fusses about it. He doesn't care about recognition or a pat on the back.

Quick story... When I was at the Marine Military Academy and it was the end of my junior year, it came time to buy our class rings. MMA class rings are rare. They are like graduating from a small yet well-known college. Anyways, my roommate, Rivers, did not have the means to purchase one. But when they arrived a month later, Rivers had a ring to wear. The gifter asked to remain anonymous. But it was my pop. That's the kind of guy he is. So if you see him, thank him, and hope that you may get the chance to hear one of his quotes.

Back to the book... Going to treatment in Houston dried my sorry ass up. Little did I know, in drying up I learned that my mental health

The Story

was not up to standards, you would say. Stupid bipolar. When one is dual diagnosed, it is hard to accept it and find the starting point to recover. For me, I didn't know what was right or wrong to say; I didn't know if I said something bad. I would have to be committed (because there was some scary shit up there that I didn't want to give up). We will get into that later...

Anyways, 30 days came and went. I was released back into society with basic tools of recovery and a hunger for narcotics to match. Let's just say I had to "pawn" my tools for a while. Once again, the scotch and pilsner ran wild. I was drinking again. And once the drinking started, the crack rock was soon to follow. You see, I wasn't a wake up and take a hit of crack kind of guy. No, I had to drink first. And once the alcoholic demon got on my shoulder and did his thing, I was walking down streets you would only see in movies, looking for that little expensive rock of cocaine. Ah, the things we do, eh? You know what I'm talking about...

This run lasted about a year. I was lying to my parents about where I was. The paychecks I did make were gone within 8 hours of getting it in my hand. I stole and I pawned. All this in the name of what I thought a good time was. It was nothing more than booze and drugs. My life sucked. I knew it, and so did everyone else. I was on probation at the time. I should have been locked up sooooo many times. My angel must have been watching over me. I was never piss tested once. Hell, I even showed up high to my appointments on either crack or powder cocaine. She never blinked. She must have hated her job.

Fast forward 4 years and four treatment centers later... I believe at this point I really wanted to quit my chaotic life style. The good news was since I'd ran out of money, I was crack free for over a month. The bad news was that the scotch ran like a natural spring fountain. But I tried to change. I was living in a long-term residential treatment center in downtown Houston. I really believe that this center is where I made my first honest attempt at recovery. It was run by two friends of mine named Victor and Gail. They were perfect for each other, and were perfect for the center. Victor looked like a miniature Jack Nicholson. The way he flailed his arms or gave you that Jack smile of his, you couldn't help but laugh and respect the man at the same time.

I think this was also the first time my alter ego didn't get into the picture. I was actually happy for the first time. I made friends, and my family was starting to talk to me again. I still fed off of this attention because let's face it . . . I was still codependent.

I wanted to impress my parents very dearly. But at 6 months into this center, I was accused of using and ordered a piss test. How dare they think that about a chronic addict who lies and only has 6 months sober!?! Oh, come on . . . you've thought this way before. We think after 30 days, all is forgiven for 30 years of addiction and pain. Be real. So being the weasel I was, I had a backdoor escape plan in case something didn't go my way. I knew I was gonna piss clean anyways, but I left in the middle of the day by means of a friend and dancer . . . let's call her "Sasha." It took 3 hours from the time I packed my shit and was relocated until I was drinking my first glass of scotch. All over resentment. Pathetic, eh? I would love to sit here and write that it was Victor and the center's fault, and I would love to say that nothing good ever came out of that place . . . but I would be lying to you. I learned a great deal and if it wasn't for the encouragement from Victor, I would never had had the nerve to meet my biological mother.

This is a topic that was taboo for me growing up. A lot of you out there who were adopted might know what I am saying. So he helped me figure it was time to deal with the emotions and feelings and a possible closure. So I went to the agency from where I was adopted, and enrolled in a class to deal with issues. After 2 weeks of therapy and a lot of role playing, it was decided that a search for my mother would be made. They warned me that she may not want to meet me. I was so proud of myself for getting this far with the search, I was already mentally prepared. So, guess what happens? That's right, I met my mother. After they gave me her name and address, I called, crying of course, and set up a place and time to meet. That night, in front of an AA meeting, I hugged Ruthie for the first time. She was late, just like a woman. But I didn't care. It was like looking into a mirror. Almost immediately, questions I had were answered right there. She held me so tight, I thought we were one. I had found my mom. You would think my journey and quest had been reached. Well, think again. It had only begun because, unfortunately, the visit was too hard on her, and she fled. Those were the two most magical weeks a person could ever ask for, though. I learned about her alcoholism, being a single mother in the '70s, and that her being a minister's daughter would not be good for me. She told me of the love she never let go of for me. All this fueled me for the journey to continue for as long as it would take. No one will ever take her away from me. I will kill or die for either of my mothers. Believe that. I am a big believer in family. I may not act like it, but if harm comes to those I love, I get mad. I have a decent way of handling my anger issues that I have learned. But the hurting of my family is where I draw the line. So . . . nobody do that, deal?

Back to our visit. . . Unfortunately, being with me was too hard on my mom and she fled. Once again . . . alone. Once again . . . abandonment issues. And at the same time, my other mother, I find out, was sad and depressed cause she thought I wouldn't need her anymore. She couldn't have been more wrong. This is the woman who raised me, loved me, fixed me, taught me, and showed me the way to adulthood. No doubt about it, she is my mom. So remember when we were at the part of the story where I had left the treatment center? Let's get back to that, shall we? After I settled in at my friend's house, it was only a matter of hours before I had drugs, liquor, and a real bad idea. Now, fast forward 2 weeks. I stole a certain amount of money to smoke a certain amount of stuff for over a certain amount of time. Are you the type of dope fiend that would steal from your buddy and then go help them look for it? Me too. I still don't know if she ever thought I did it. Anyways, she got into trouble with the property management and had to move. I pulled a few strings and got us an apartment where I had once lived. You would have loved it. It was built in the '60s and was tropical. Anyways, I was still lazy and uncaring. My best friend to this day still loves to point it out . . . if you ever get a chance to, fart in an elevator.

But I was also a genius. Being a lazy, drunken, no good bum can take a lot outta man. There is a lot of work involved. First, you have to make sure your drug supply stays close by, then, there's the skill of hiding booze all over the house and also trying to remember where you hid it the next day. There are the lies one has to keep up with and then the fine art of somehow maintaining a false sense of Zen when around people who love you. Do you know there are people who go to Ivy League colleges to learn how to multitask like a dope fiend? Yeah—business degrees. I am a firm believer that companies should hire a couple of recovering addicts. Not by force, but by knowing what they can produce.

You hear about beautiful fundraisers for breast cancer and sick puppies, but what do the addicts get? A reality show with famous people. Oh well. It beats getting locked up in an insane asylum. If you haven't read the Big Book, you probably wouldn't have gotten that last part.

Deep down there was an overwhelming sense of shame for what I had become. I still have trouble looking in a mirror to this day. And when I was really depressed and guilt ridden, I quit talking to my family. I mean, completely disconnect. My dad would have to hire private investigators to find me at times.

One day, my hot dancer roommate bought a keg of beer on a whim. I assumed it was for a party but when she set down only two red plastic cups, I knew I was in trouble. My liver knew it too. In between passing out, we drank for 3 days straight before we both quit. Oh yeah, there are stories. Like the one, during a blackout, where we apparently drove to Sam Houston State University so she could see one of her boyfriends. When we woke up in a dorm room, we had no recollection on how we got there. I thought, my God, I need to stabilize myself and get a goddamn drink! Five days and a quarter of a keg left, there was a knock at my door.

Without looking through the peek hole, I flung the door open in a fashion so horrible, you would pray that I was only drunk. Standing in the doorway was my father. Through my life, I've seen my father mad, sad, confused, and relieved. But never at once. He stared me dead in the eye and said, "I don't know whether to hit you or hug you!" And with that said, he turned around and walked away. It was at that exact moment that I realized my addiction doesn't just affect me, it affects everyone around me.

And with that said, it was a matter of time before she threw me out on my ass. One month to be exact. I had met other people who had lived in the same complex, and when I got the boot I moved in with them. This time, we all got evicted. There was one last shot that I could pull outta my sleeve. I had met a woman who lived there who was a raging alcoholic and sex addict. I hit the motherload. And, I had found someone as sick as me.

The Story

This "relationship" went on for about 3 weeks. I was already planning my next move.

I had a dear friend up in Spring, Texas, who I could call. He quickly came over and brought me back with him. He fed me, he housed me, and he even gave me a job. But to look at me was to vomit. I had to detox to a functioning level. So a joint and a six pack later, I was cleaned up and selling men's and women's perfume. You've seen us. We are the Mormons of fast pitched sales in strip mall parking lots. Say what you will about us, but some of these people can make up to a thousand dollars a week. I admire that. I learned a whole new type of sales and I loved it! Now, two things happened—I got so good I could train a guy or gal in the field by picking out the people, or "marks" that I knew would buy, and send the new hire to close the deal. And my drinking increased two twofold. I was selling and pocketing 100% of the sales profit to feed my need to drink and drug. No one ever questioned me. Management rocks! We trained and motivated the sales people in the morning and then sent them out to make us money. We stayed behind and drank beer and smoked a lot of good green herb my European boss would plop out. As bad as life was, I was good.

After 3 months of this, one night I got a wild hair up my ass to relocate to the Valley—Harlingen, Texas. The armpit of Texas. I don't know why. I talked to my so-called girlfriend at the time into driving me down to south Texas. I asked her to stay, not really wanting her to, and join me. She declined, whew, and drove away into the morning sun. Here I am homeless, alone, in another city in Texas, in the Deep South, and I'm broke. Fuck.

I have a survival technique that kicks in once my being is in distress. I adapted and improvised, hoping to overcome. I shacked up with a girl I knew when I was attending school down there. She had a house with no air conditioning, no hot water, and no electricity. All this in the middle of summer. Nice.

There was no food and I needed to drink in order to prevent detox and going into shakes. I started trading bottles of men's or women's perfume and cologne for booze and sandwiches. $30 a pop these things went for and I was reduced to Blue Ribbon and old turkey sandwiches. What a life.

One night, I got to thinking about my past and the eight treatment centers I'd attended. A whole new level of depression sank in, and it teetered on the suicidal side. During this drinking expedition, I came across a bottle of fine bourbon somehow and I drank it right out of the bottle as quickly as I could to speed up the alcohol poisoning. At the time of my blackout, I managed to call 911 and tell them what I was going to do. I said, "Tell my parents in Houston, Texas, that I love them!" I fell to the curb and fought back the rage and the alter ego of "other Wes" from coming out and destroying myself. Luckily, the ambulance came because I left the phone off of the hook and they could trace it to me laying on the curb, shaking and talking to myself. My friend talked the cops and the paramedics outta taking me away. I passed out to her taking advantage of me. Good times . . .

This friend later took a road trip and left me in the care of her good friend, "Mary C." She picked me up and we went to a fleabag motel and had a cooler of beer, a full pack of Reds, hard pack, a buzz, and the whole night. Beer flowed like the Colorado River after a rain season. We were pretty pissed and having a good time playing pool. After hours of sexual tension and flirting, we hooked up. And the best part, after we were done she got dressed and left with me still in the room for the whole night. And there was still half a cooler of beer and the adult channel. It was the first time in a long time that I had a bed, shower, clean sheets, and an A/C running on 65 degrees. God threw me a bone.

When she came back the next day, around ten-ish, I was already drunk as shit. She took me to Mexico to continue the party and I got even more drunk and blacked out. I came to with her arms around my neck and her kissing me. Apparently, I asked her to marry me while in Mexico. It was pretty cool for a common law marriage. I got a new start, a chance to re-prove myself to my parents, and this new woman in my life. We kinda learned each other as we went along. For example, she likes to snuggle. I liked to get really drunk and come home at 3:00 a.m. and throw up all over the bathroom.

So as you see, there were challenges along the way. And what a ride it was. Two-and-a-half years later, we called it quits. Well, I called it quits. Actually, I got drunk and walked away from her and her mother standing in the front yard begging me to come back. Now before you go off and

The Story

start thinking what a dick I was, know that I was the only provider for a woman who did nothing for work other than be a phone sex operator. We had a crappy apartment in the Valley and my in-laws polished the Catholic Ghost in everything I did. I hate to be cornered.

I went to a treatment center for help because I went on a 5-day bender. My insurance would only pay for a 2-day detox. So 2 days later, I was on the street sleeping in a dumpster and eating food out of trash cans.

Yup, that's right. I slept in dumpsters, ate out of other ones, walked the streets to stay warm, and when I could, I would drink myself to sleep. Now a humble man with no signs of an altar to pray to or any ego in sight, I called my old friend I had left. Alex came to pick me up and bring me back to his house to sober up and hopefully get help. It is good to hope. I'd lost mine.

I bounced from couch to couch until I raked up enough money, a decent job, an apartment, and about the weight of a single grain of sand's worth of trust. It was in a nice part of town, but although I was hanging around sober people 24/7, I still didn't do the twelve steps needed to learn how to live. Because in the end, no matter how many groups break down the Big Book and try to find messages within its pages, all it is, is a guide to show us how to live. Plain and simple. So, go live. . .

Anyways, since I didn't work the steps at all, it was only a matter of time before I went completely insane and drank. After 6 months of being dry and having drinking and using dreams every night, I literally told my roommates I was going to go out and drink and drug. I drank as if 6 months was only 6 minutes sober, without a care in the world. And then, within 3 hours of hard drinking, I was smoking crack in a Chevron bathroom with two other people. If you wonder how long it took me to make the decision to use, snap your fingers together and it still isn't fast enough. When I got home, all my friends were in my apartment waiting for me. I wanted to fight them all and try to make a run for it. I wanted to. I didn't. Instead I went into self-preservation and submitted to going back to another detox. This one was free. And in a bad part of town. Crap. I sat on a bench in a 24-hour AA club waiting to see if they would let me have a bed to live on for 2 weeks. Oh, did I mention I was detoxing, coming down off of crack, and the temperature outside wailed over a hundred degrees? Yeah, nice. I finally got a bed and began my newest adventure. This place should have been condemned. And the guy they chose to run the house thought scare tactics would keep everyone sober in the house. I guess bullying men into sobriety is somewhere tucked away within the pages of the Big Book. It was miserable and hot, and I almost wished I was in a jail cell. At least I'd have A/C and semi-decent food. But I made it.

From there, I went to the Salvation Army in downtown Houston. I resided there for 2 weeks before a psychiatric bipolar episode got my butt thrown out for scaring the help.

I was a hot, sick mess. I didn't know which way was up, nor could I differentiate my ass from a hole in the ground. I didn't know what to do. I called my pops and he took me to a psych hospital where I could get help. After the standard 24-hour suicide watch, they moved me to residential on the second floor. All I saw was black. All I could think was black. And the weight on my shoulders mixed with the pins in my stomach made every thought hurt even more. I wished I was dead.

This is the part in my story where I have to tell you that God does work miracles in mysterious ways. When you least expect a gift in life is when God decides to give you one. He gave me an angel disguised in women's clothing. And she was the most beautiful angel God had to give. She'll deny it to this day if you ask her, but she saved my life. She helped me change my ways and see that I have potential. I could not stand to not be around her. I wanted to inhale her soul and absorb her love. This angel came into my life and inscribed her name on my arm and my heart: Kell. She asked me to keep her out of this book, and I will respect her personal life. But because of her, I am who I am today.

Against my family's advice, or as us addicts know it—AMFA—I moved to Austin with her and a set of beautiful twins, who were aged 4 at the time. Werm and Haylebear were so cute then. We began our new life together. This was the first and only time I had believed so deeply about something or someone that I didn't care what others and my family thought. Once settled in, I started a ritual that would happen every morning for almost 90 days. When we would wake up, I would say, "Good morning. I love you. Will

The Story

you marry me today?" and every morning she would reply, "Good morning. I love you too. No I won't marry you today." Good thing I'm persistent. It would pay off for me sooner than I thought.

On October 17, 2000, I was bit by a brown recluse spider on top of my femoral artery. Kell was also bit . . . six times on the back of her legs. I was going to die unless they got me in an ER and stopped the infection right there and then. Turns out the little spider was carrying a parasite, so now I was contagious as well. I was lying in my hospital bed, dying without a certain antibiotic I so desperately needed, and Kell said, "If you live, I will marry you Wesley." I had hope. I smiled. I talked to God and said, "Listen here. You and me, we gotta work it out. You really don't want me up there causing a lot of ruckus and I'm not ready to go. I haven't used up my nine lives I got now." Doesn't it seem we always bargain with him when it's something we want? Well, the next morning they got the serum they needed to fix me up. As soon as I could walk, I took my soon-to-be-bride to the courthouse, hobbled up the stairs, gimped my way into the license department, and demanded a marriage license before she changed her mind! On October 21, 2000, we were married. She was my wife and I was her husband. I love that spider, damnit. You need to know that on the day of our wedding, it poured down rain all morning. She was worried for obvious reasons that our day would be ruined. Or even worse, canceled. I told her not to worry, but to have faith and trust me. The Big Guy will fix this. So she quieted down a bit, and we went to our wedding. It rained the whole way to the gazebo at the park. But when we parked and got out, the rain stopped, literally from the time we got out of our car till the minister pronounced us "man and wife." Afterward, we walked back to the car and once we'd got in, it rained again. And a lot harder.

To cliff-hang, or not to cliff-hang? Now, after all that, you may be waiting for me to write something like: Happily ever after, right? Wrong! Life didn't get easier. My addiction was still a case of the hot, sick progression and I tried and tried to keep it at bay. I swear to God. There were times when my wife and I would fight and argue about my drinking. Then there were the times when I would just leave for hours or days at a time. The addiction rolled on, destroying everything in my path. Lies were told to get money and stuff I needed from family and friends. The trust I had was quickly and quietly replaced with sadness and anger. Booze was winning.

A lot more happened, but I don't want to give away my next... big thing with lots of pages and no screen or cords. I'm sure what you have read is depressing and, according to "Daffy," who had read two chapters, almost unbelievable. But it's my life, and there are others out there who have it a lot worse than I did or do now. My daddy used to say, "No matter how good a boxer you think you are, there is always someone out there who is better." I still remember this, but I believe the same saying can spin the other way. An addict's point of view, no matter how bad we think we got it, is that there is someone out there who is going through a lot worse right now.

There are a lot of great times I've had growing up, too. I was blessed with a beautiful and funny daughter, I have learned and laughed along the way, and the hole I dug doesn't seem so deep anymore.

Update: My biological mother is doing great and we have reunited.

CHAPTER 4

ADMITTED

I wrote this chapter the MINUTE I realized that if I started at the beginning then sooner or later there would be an end. It was a good feeling. It is also quite educational, informative, and a little preachy. It is what it is, so take it or leave it. Suck on that. It was the first phase of my new recovery. As we know, us addicts will take hold of this new life and thump it till they die with 40 years sober or they taper off. I tapered.

Rat & Pig Rule!
"We admitted we were powerless over alcohol,
and that our lives have become unmanageable."[1]

In this step, we have to admit, to be honest with ourselves. Some will say that this is done once we get into AA and get the sponsor to push us along. For me, I believe I took this step way out there at the end of my active addiction when I made the choice to get help. I was laid up in an ICU hospital bed with all sorts of monitors and drip bags. Four nurses looked over me and an open head wound the size of a squash ball. I had a lot of quiet time laying there on a morphine drip. I thought mostly of my behavior and evidence thereof. Twenty plus years of using and abusing, and here I am again . . . at the beginning. Is this what it has to take for me to finally get it? How much more do I have to lose? How many hospitals, charcoal breakfasts, and overdrawn accounts do I have to owe? I should have died so many times over so many years. I guess having two lives left will do that to you.

We have a bad habit of sabotaging ourselves. I have seen people, including myself, come through the doors hopeless and defeated. Once the addict gets some good sleep, a decent meal or two, and an introduction to AA locked in their head, a job comes next. We all love money. The good news is that the addict is feeling good and confident about themselves. Even their family says, "Our son is not such an asshole anymore." Everyone is happy.

The bad news is that they start to feel too good, compromise right from wrong, and blow any sober time had. My father has coined the phrase, "Shooting your self in the foot syndrome." We forget how powerless we really are. We forget how unmanageable our lives once were. And as a result, men and women will return to their lives believing that they have it under control. Why the need to live the first step all day, every day? Because it's the one we have to work 100% of the time. We have to uncover to discover the need to recover.

Bella Lugosi once said, "To be alive, to be truly alive. That would be glorious!"[2] What does this mean to you? We enter AA as a newcomer or a relapse case if we didn't die. Either way, we are spiritually dead and emotionally drained. We've kicked our own ass, are tired of it, and want help by any means possible and available. Someone early on in my recovery once told me that it is easy to get clean off of booze and drugs. It's the staying clean that's the bitch. But if we put half the energy of our addiction into getting sober, we have a good chance of long-term sobriety. Honesty is the antidote. And a self-proclaimed AA guru once told me no matter what, just don't pick up. If we don't look for the drink or drug then the addiction won't come knocking at the door.

Take the first step forward and admit there is a problem. No one can tell you or persuade you that you are an addict. For me, when I started this journey years ago, I thought my problem was the white powdery substance called cocaine. I wanted to quit, yet I didn't. I always had a backout plan just in case. It took another year before I quit the stuff, and another 6 months to quit looking through a peep hole. But my drinking was out of control and I was completely blind to being an alcoholic. I mean seriously, I thought I didn't have a problem . . . even with three DWIs under my belt. It took the help from a dear old friend of mine named Pat, also known to me as

Pablo, to get me to see the light. He had me write out all of my alcohol related run-ins, wrecks involving my car and others, and arrests on paper so I could see in black and white where I have been blind and wrong. Ouch.

The weird thing about being bipolar is that it turns you into a depressive mess for most of the time. In no way is having a mental disease a scapegoat for me. But the fact is, my mental health does play a part in my own deterioration of following society's rules. I drank. I attended meetings. I attended meetings both hammered and high. And even though I comprehended every aspect of the first step and how to apply it, I still acted out with my "SEM" way of a lifestyle. I thought with enough AA knowledge in my head I could take control of my life and my drinking. Haha!

Much, much later, I finally let go of my control and let God do what he does best: lead. And when I did, I believed. I had hope and faith to finally understand it was a work in progress. So I learned something new, and found great relief in this new knowledge. If it was my way, He would have to come down from Heaven above and flick my forehead which would absorb His power. But alas, it was going to take some good old-fashioned work. Which was something I really did not like to do. Nor would I, for many years to come. But for now, recovery came first. So I got a sponsor, vocalized the first step every morning, and lived a spiritual life to the fullest of my ability.

We love to complicate things and analyze challenges. Not so much for stubbornness reasons, but because we, as alcoholics, are very intelligent people. Seriously, find a recovering addict or drunk and ask them what they do and I bet it's skilled and incredible! But since we are such smarty pants, we look for shortcuts and loopholes to crawl through. Big secret... When in AA, play dumb. Do not take offense. And if you do, poop on you. AA is a form of humility. The dumber we stay, the sober we get. And, in turn, the recovery is better. But please take note: do not become a doormat for suggestions. For Christ's sake, set boundaries. When I was new, I took so much from everyone I had no idea which way was up and which way was Scottish. Like a normal drinker, I had to take "long-termer's" advice in moderation. And once I did that, I could focus on the goal and get through one day at a time (as my buddy, the Rev. would say... pause).

First Step Prayer:

Dear Lord, I admit that I am powerless over my addiction. I admit that my life is unmanageable when I try to control it. Help me this day to understand the true meaning of powerlessness. Remove from me all denial of my addiction. Amen.

Sniff. Brings a tear to yer eye doesn't it? That is straight from what I like to call "The Bible." Also known as The Big Book. If you want to learn how to live, I highly suggest that you read the B. B. as soon as you are done reading mine. I owe my life to the writings of Bill W. and Dr. Bob. Without them, this book would never have been brought to light.

Not all of us will need an inpatient setting. I did, and am since really grateful for the experience. But others are able to walk into a meeting and stay sober for the rest of their lives. What are the pros and cons of stepping out of your comfort zone in recovery? Well, you have the freedom to choose which meetings and what times you would like to go. There are a gazillion meetings in your area. Shop around and find the one you like. Take your time, it's your recovery. Don't settle. It you get bored with your home group, move on! For those of you who are not familiar with our drunk slang, home groups are where you can pay dues, be on the committee, and help when they need it. I used to fix the A/C for my group. John(s) are good people up there in Austin.

Once you are settled in, start getting phone numbers from other people in the group. Some will say to only get the number from the same sex people, but why? I say get as many numbers, both male and female, as you can get. Everyone deserves to listen and maybe save your life.

A relaxed schedule can go either way. But since we are relating it to the pros side, a schedule of this caliber can (A) reduce stress, and (B) dramatically reduce anxiety. It's all about scheduling a daily event planner and personal planner to take out the stress and anxiety or bring it to a level easier to deal with. In early recovery, it is highly suggested that we go to as many meetings as we can within the first 90 days. I personally do not agree with this. When veterans of AA tell the newcomer, "Ninety meetings in 90 days," it sets that newbie up for failure. What if they cannot make it on Monday nights because of a babysitter challenge? Anxiety and depression for failure reasons start to whelm up and consume our thinking. So, what did I do? I drank. I say try to make 90 in 90 and if you cannot, then that's okay too. Some people need two, one, or even three a day to help with their disease. Others can get away with three a week. It's not a cult. No one says you have to live in the rooms of AA.

If you have not lost your job to the addiction, good for you. But know that you are somewhere on the "yet" list. Believe me, they have their eye on you. It is important to have a balance in your personal life and recovery life. Can you make it work? Is it possible to hit a meeting before you go into work, or is it better for you to hit one during the lunch hour? You are responsible for your recovery. What are you willing to put in?

What are you going to take out? Sometimes, I used to think everyone was breathing down my neck to get sober and go, go, go to meetings. But they weren't. Eh, for the most part they weren't. I made a mountain out of a molehill. Don't do that. Oh, also don't put others and situations before your recovery. It is the easiest way to lose focus. So . . . big no no.

Want a cool way to stay sober and help others coming into the program? Go share your story at a treatment center. Even though you may have never been in a residential treatment center to get sober, you still have a message to share. Be quick to recognize the help you can provide to those less fortunate. You may even pick up a sponsee that has what you want. It is a God blast when you leave and are aware of how you feel.

Another thing one can do is when the meeting is over and all your friends are leaving, is stay. Stick around and get phone numbers. Meet strange and unusual people—and become friends. We are so quick to jump out of our seats and bolt for the door as soon as the chip system has been done (milestones for us in recovery). I've done it. We all have. But you don't have to do it every time. Make coffee, clean up after, do something for no reason. What's it going to hurt? Invest a little more into a solid recovery and all it can do is help. Do not get me wrong. I recommend that fellowship outside the walls off AA be as active as it can. Going out and doing whatever with your AA friends is important on a social and psychological level. Movies, pool, dinner, dating . . . you name it, it is all good and healthy. It helps establish us into the world again. If there is something wrong, then it is easier for us to go into a meeting, talk about it, and see if anyone in there might have a solution we can take back out into the world and apply.

As we all know, when we get sober, it is important to relearn as much as possible. Our mental growth stopped with the first drink or hit. Never stop learning!

Integrity: When you are alone in a room, you fart, and you still say, "excuse me."

Self-reliance. The beat up and stained version of Webster's dictionary defined it as, "trust, dependence, or confidence." Be careful with this one. When you believe that you can do it by yourself, you probably can't. With self-reliance, you can be sure to have confidence when it comes to doing the next right thing. This type of addict is my favorite. These people usually become sponsors and also members of their home group. There is also a distinct notion of assurance in their life to jump to the challenge and overcome obstacles. God love 'em.

Being God-centered and believing that "He can and we can't" will elevate us to a new chapter in recovery. In doing so, it is very important to remember that He can only lead us halfway. It is up to us and our faith to find energy to finish the journey we so willingly started. Get accountable. Call your sponsor. And when a crisis does come up, use the tools given and His guidance to reach out and communicate via phone, text, meeting, or one-on-one time with another addict. Faith without manpower is unacceptable. Do the work and you will be rewarded. Period.

One of the last pros I wish to discuss is the ability to attend an outpatient program. These programs are nice because they allow you to work around your schedule.

These programs run anywhere from 30 days up to 90 days. And from personal experience, I know some outpatient programs run longer. Much, much longer. If you decide to follow this course of recovery, it is important that you know not to hold back any emotions or truths that are hiding deep within. You are going to be in a safe environment and I encourage you to share. Plus, due to the Americans with Disabilities

Act, what you say is stored away secured. It means what you say in the rooms of the outpatient is confidential, top secret. The only time that can be broken by a counselor is if a child is involved and harmed, or if any self-threat of harm results in suicide. Use the groups. If there are issues too personal to share in group, then schedule a one-on-one with your counselor. Now, to back up. The reason I spent such a long, long, long time in outpatient is I never took anything whatsoever about recovery seriously. I would barely scratch the surface of my issues, drink as soon as I got out of outpatient, drink before outpatient, and never call anyone to hang out with; basically, I'd be high constantly and just didn't care. You follow this path, and a nice big police file with your name all over it will be waiting for you. Thank God I had a counselor who never gave up on me. If you go in and do what needs to be done, then good things await. If you resist, use, and lie, then your misery is gladly refunded to you at the front door.

I have seen brothers and sisters come into the program and only do the basics and riot outside meetings. They do fine for a while, but eventually fall back into their old ways and patterns. If only they used some spiritual guidance, a phone call, and a meeting. But right there is the difference, I think. I have sat in enough rooms of AA and other recovery related rooms to see who is there and who isn't, who were the relapsers and who gabbed the most. Sure enough over time, when someone went out, it appeared there was disgust in their faces as they talked about "this person" who relapsed. Why? I see someone who fell and needs a hand. They see a drunk who's going to rob you blind. In my other group when I or someone else went out, they completely shut you out. And they turn your family on you and say that what you are doing to your family is a sin! And then you are alone when you need someone, anyone, the most.

With all this talk about pro this and pro that, here comes the cons. CONS! Hahaha ... get it? These are guaranteed to hold you back from a true spiritual recovery if you follow your "own" path to evil. The first one is structure. This is good applied to everyday life. I still need it today. But in recovery, if there is no structure, then we are lost. As addicts and alcoholics, we are carefree about the lives we live and daily activities.

We had no time schedules as a kid. There were no appointments that needed to be kept, not much to commit to, and we tried to make it a habit not to be somewhere when we were asked to. Growing up, we relied on our parents to do this for us. They told us what to wear, how to act, what to eat, and how much to eat, and when to go to bed. In our active addiction, we cannot admit that we need help. Even with the littlest things. This means the simplest things too. This is why, for me, going at recovery by myself and acting out is like a child whose parents have gone out for the evening. But the evening lasted 28 years. Like I said before, I went to a military academy. Even though on the weekends there was a large amount of drinking, border crossing, beach bunnies, and psychedelics at the academy, during the week there was a lot of structure in the military persuasion. And as a result, I managed to graduate with a diploma. So with structure comes accomplishments. See the path?

So, there it is, the educational part of the book. I had planned to write more cons to fulfill an argument. But I don't think cons are really that important. If a mistake is made, change.

Besides, it's only my opinion. Your program is yours. You can do it your way, but wherever we go, there we are.

CHAPTER 5
THE WORLD THROUGH MY EYES

In 1993, I was completely blown over with cocaine and alcohol consumption. I was officially numb. I blocked out every emotion I had. I pushed away anyone who was in my life. Flat-out, the world only revolved around me. The only sobering thoughts I had were: "How to get more?" "Where was I gonna get the money for it today?" and "What lie could I muster up to get you to get me what I needed?" Now, lemme back up a wee bit. You see, growing up in my family, we never discussed anything. Only anger. Don't hate on mom and pops, they did a great job. It was the way they were raised and in turn, raised Patrick and me. This was very common with my generation. We are as normal as the next. But as my mom says, "What is normal when it comes to families?" You ever been to a Functioning Families Anonymous meeting? Me neither.

So, in my world, everything I was doing seemed alright to me. I was only hurting myself. I wasn't happy. Some nights, I would cry myself to sleep, high on drugs of course, praying to God to either help me or kill me. He did neither one. So I thought. He did something with my parents in which they were now motivated with a fire under their asses later that year—Bam! I was finally introduced to recovery and my inner being. You get what you pray for, but how you get your prayer is a different matter altogether now isn't it?

So, in the fall of 1993, after a night of heavy cocaine use, my mom approached me. I'm laying on the couch in a leg cast and she gave me an ultimatum. Either pack my shit and get out of her house, or meet a gentleman who would be over shortly to talk about getting sober and getting help. Fearing the obvious has a lot of power. Knowing in the back of my mind I was not even close to giving up the drugs, I lied through my teeth and said I'd meet him and get the help I so desperately needed.

Here's the problem: since I had no emotions, I used and manipulated my mom to get what I wanted, caused my father to worry and have clinical depression, drove my only brother away from me, and after all that, I still didn't have a care in the world. Just tuned it out. Now what you have here is a family that's unwilling to communicate. It has never been a "selfish disease," it is a "Family disease." When we go out and use and then throw up and pass out in some rundown house . . . "we" aren't the ones who are only getting hurt. Mom, pops, my brother—it affected them too.

I was blind. I was unwilling to see the pain. It is quite amazing how blind we get when we "self-absorb" over our addiction. I swear, I honestly did not know I was hurting my family. Unfortunately, this realization did not come over night. Nor within the first year and a half of my recovery. Do you remember earlier when I said I wasn't ready to give it up?

I wasn't ready to give it up. I started recovery with an outpatient program. In the morning I would get up and go regardless whether I had either been sober or drunk or really, really high. I had no choice, ergo no shame.

You know when someone in AA tells you, "Ah man, shoulda got right the first time." First, I wanna punch that man in the mouth and second, well I wish I would have. By 1994, I had several convictions under my belt. D'oh!

It's hard to judge who will get sober in AA, NA, CA, and OA and who will not. Why? Cause no one knows who's going to make it and who can't, or won't. All I can say is some of us do, and some of us do it later. I was so jealous of those who could stay sober and make something of their life. I wanted to set fire to their rabbit cages! But no matter what, I kept going and never quit. Never. Through lies, relapses, jail time, and frustrations, I just kept going. So many times, I wanted to quit and eat a Nike full of Xanax, lie down, and never wake up. I never gave up. I saw happiness in simple things: TV, nature, *Pearls Before Swine*, Homer, and my daughter's word, "Fight." I believe even with those touching words it still took me 2 years to muster up 30 days of sobriety. And it was about 2 seconds after that I felt truly happy for the first time. But it didn't last long. I was white knuckling it. I didn't do any step work, use a sponsor, go to any meetings, talk to anyone about my day-to-day activities, or connect with God.

But I stuck with it, and soon I learned to talk about my feelings and to share my emotions in a way that didn't belittle me or cause me to shut down. As a result, and as time went on, I wasn't so angry. I could talk to my parents. I could reestablish some form of communication with my brother. I could start to right the wrongs in my life. And the best and coolest part? I now started to remember the night before, when I go to bed and wake up sober. The feelings did not happen overnight, you know. Back then, I could turn my emotions on and off with the flip of a switch. Kinda like a stage actor. Being bipolar basically intensified these emotions. I've seen it in others identical to myself. For me, when I'm on top of the world, things are going to be good. But because I am cursed, I have to "Shoot myself in the foot a couple times." Meaning I sabotage my happiness. It boils down to a fear of success. When things started to get good in my life, I would get the itch, and find a way to ruin whatever it is I was doing. Whew. Tiring. Let's back up to the bipolar and mental health aspect of me, myself, and monkeys. This is not a "cop out" by any means. But it does play a factor in my everyday life. If you remember reading back in this book about the time in the psych ward, then you read notes that were written while a massive bipolar attack was in full swing. My craziest thinking produced the most sane thinking in plain black and white.

Today I am who I am and completely comfortable with my past. I went though the shame and blah, blah, blah. It is time to live.

You want to live? Get out there.

CHAPTER 6
WESLEY'S CUBE

Completely sober, addicts of every type and caliber, including myself, are the most interesting people in the world. But since I was told to only talk about myself, and since this big, sweaty man has a pistol pressed against my cheek, I will tell you about a person a lot of people like to call, Nice Wes. When there are no chemicals in my body, I am a pleasant person to be around. I am kind, funny, outgoing, and responsible. But for every good side, there has to be a dark. Whatever chemical is introduced into my body, I change. I become a whole different person. I become nonresponsive, angry, uncaring to anyone, and what my ex-wife would classify me as, an "asshole."

But back to the being completely sober part—I am a good person who is helpful, caring, loving, considerate, and hard working. And since this book has been an ongoing process of intensive inner research and general time, I had a chance to do something I hardly did at that time, I listened to myself for the first time. And by this, I mean my INNER self. I must remind you, the reader, what you read is true, not made-up head games. These thoughts you will read come right outta my thought process when I am either depressed or excited.

One night, during an emotional breakdown having been discharged from a dual diagnosis wing of a hospital, I laid on the floor in the bathroom and finely tuned into my inner thoughts and workings. I closed my eyes and saw myself spinning in a circle until I came to a stop and saw myself staring right back at myself in my reflection. There were two of me, but one was pure as the driven snow and the other was evil in the purest. He smiles and uncrossed his legs, bent over, and when he talked to me, I knew at that moment that "SEM" was gone forever.

And what he said to me was everything I've ever known. "You're a complete loser! You have no purpose in life, no direction! You'll be broke your whole life! You're not worth loving! You can't even overdose right! Your brother made something of himself—why can't you? God made you an addict because he likes to watch you suffer!"

And then he said something that really caught my attention. "Well you might as well sit back and let me do what it is I do best. We can attach onto each other and live our lives in wonder." I opened my eyes and felt my heart stop. Just for a second. But long enough to make me cry and shiver at the same time. It was at that moment I realized the Wesley I knew had been poisoned, dismantled, and reconstructed into pure, horrific evil: this other Wes.

Now since I knew there was no way I was going to get any sleep that night, I got up and went for a walk. I started thinking about the beginning, before the drugs, before the booze. Who was I?

Growing up, I had every boy's dream of what parents should be. They instilled values unto me. They stayed up late helping me with homework. They attended my sports games and they loved it! Birthdays and Christmases with my family were incredible. But like any family and their cycle, "hand me down emotions" ran thick in the Brann Clan. I never heard a lot of "I love you" and when punishments were being handed out, they were fair and just. It was the time to serve out the sentence given by mom, the beatings were very 1970s. Couldn't get away with that now. Kid will make a movie. Ha! But you know what? That was okay too. I took a good beating with a belt, nylon cord, nylon cord covered in plastic, a hand, and one time a wooden spoon. That was my favorite. I love moms and pops. They did the best they could with what they had. So, when challenges started to crop up, we all scattered.

Now before any of you start to judge mom and pop on their teaching method, don't. Listen first. There was a hidden blessing to come out of my disease with alcohol and cocaine and well . . . whatever you got. Everyone changed inside. Slowly at first. Some quicker than others, but it did happen.

My love and respect for my moms and pops has intensified a hundred-fold since 1993. My mother has ritually attended two meetings a week for the past 18 years. She holds the proud rank of "black belt Al-Anon." Pops spends his free time driving a small bus from church to poor neighborhoods and picks up kids to take them to a church-funded afterschool program. He does this 5 days a week, 9 months out of the year. Also, we have opened a new door to our relationship in the communication department. Our way of saying "I love you" differs. It's through our actions. And they are understood.

But who was I? Somewhere along the way, a different way of thinking about who I was replaced it all. And while I walked, I was beginning to understand that figuring this out is going to be like putting together a thousand-piece jigsaw puzzle. And first I had to turn all the pieces of the "jigsaw" over to the same side. Only problem is that all the pieces are the same size and same color.

I started thinking about fear, poor self-esteem, and every little bad thing I have ever done wrong. Where would I start? How to begin? I didn't know it at the time, but it had already begun to change. Change is like that; sometimes it is so small that we do not know if it is even happening. You look down, and you've got a piece of the puzzle already fixed in place.

I was on a trip to see my daughter. I got into town early, so I had to wait till she got home from school to see her. Finally, school got out and I went to go pick her up. My ex pulled up in front of the school and we walked up to the front door. I was depressed earlier and when she saw me and I saw her, it all went away. She ran into my arms and held me longer than she normally does. In that instant connection, I felt love. Warm, unconditional love a father can only know from their 6-year-old daughter or son.

And at that moment, holding back the tears, I realized I had the first piece connected in my internal puzzle—to be the best damn father I could be to that little girl. I held her in my arms, drowned out the rest of the world, and walked back to the car with her feet dangling left to right. I couldn't let go of the hug. Here's my journal entry for that wonderful day with my daughter:

"Today went on and on and I was truly happy. We got to be goof balls having idiotic fun throughout the entire afternoon. And as today came to a purple end, and it was post-homework time and pre-bed time, I had an idea unfold. Normally she'll pick out a book and I'll read it to her as she falls asleep. Actually, it's like three books. But tonight, I suggested a new route. We should make up our own story. And it didn't stop there. We got out some paper, markers, and colored pencils and drew out our story. I divided the paper into six squares like a comic book and explained to Bethy that we would come up with a story, she'd draw the pictures, and I would write out the captions we both would create. Forty minutes later, we had our first page made and it was good.

And we will do another page tomorrow, and then the day after that, and so on.

And wouldn't you know it, I ended up finding another piece of my internal puzzle tonight—imagination and creation. These are probably the most important two I used growing up. And it took a six-year-old to show me the way, not a therapist.

I'm slowly beginning to learn that answers are everywhere and in everything. Sometimes it takes a little longer to spot 'em, but they are there. When we ask God to help us, He does."

CHAPTER 7
THE DEADLY COMBINATION

No one wants to be an alcoholic. Hell, to this day, I have yet to find a single volunteer. But like roulette, sooner or later we take that gamble, or first drink, and some of us win and the rest of us lose. I guess by now you figured it out that I lost.

Man, I crapped out. It started when I was shipped off to military school. By my own choice, thank you. I had no idea it was the beginning of the end for me. With my personality and wanting to adapt so bad . . . God! I'd find the drunkest son of a bitch I could and make friends the only way I learned how, "Tip the bottle and pour me out!" We drank a lot. But while I was throwing my guts up behind a dumpster at 2:00 a.m., I knew I was a part of something cool, a fraternity of pukers and hangovers.

It was a matter of time before I found someone at the academy who would change the equation and take the psychedelic high to a level only a few hundred thousand have ever seen and lived to tell the tale. And if it couldn't get more accessible, he was from my home town. May God have mercy on our souls.

Anyways, back to the point at hand . . .

My friend turned me onto a drug known as MDMA. Better known on the club scene as Ecstasy. And being who and what I am, I instantly fell in love with this XTC, this new dimension, this . . . new way of life! This cocktail of X, booze and well, me in general, shared a borderline death-wish lifestyle for the next 5 years. During which time, I was not able to gain weight due to the large amount of XTC I was consuming. I was 5'10 and weighed in at 124 lbs. I was Calvin Klein's wet dream. I remember sitting on Todd's balcony and thinking, "It can't get much better than this."

The Deadly Combination

Cocaine did for me what the cell phone did for the human race—it made life a whole lot easier to deal with. When initially introduced to this drug, it was once or twice a month. Very common for us addicts. Then to once or twice a week. Again, not uncommon for us. By 1992 summer of destruction, it was a $300 dollar a day habit! Okay, now it's getting odd. I was hooked and this white powder had my soul. It called, I came. Whenever and by however. Not too proud of that one. And with all of this information I have been telling you all, I was completely in denial. Oh, I knew there was a problem with the booze, but my addict brain just turned on the denial filter and as a result, the use increased and my misery tripled. And so, I stayed stuck that way for many, many years to follow.

There have been so many combinations of narcotics, pharmaceuticals and toxins running through my veins, that when it came time for me to adapt again when I got into a relationship, Benzo(s) were gonna have to do. It's not easy hiding crack cocaine use around a wife and kids. So I improvised, overcame, and adapted. Xanax, Soma, and anything else colorful got shoveled down my throat.

If you haven't sat there reading this and said, "Good Lord" or "What happened?" by now, here's your chance. The use of these pills put me in ICU five times and nearly killed me twice. I wish I could tell you I learned something from this, but shortly thereafter, I ate a handful of pills, got behind a wheel of my wife's new car, and ran it right into a pole. A pole not even 10 feet from a restaurant. God blast if I've ever seen one. Another time, after getting out of Cameron County House of Corrections, I ate a handful of pills, chased 'em with two cans of Foster's, blacked out, and cracked the back of my head open on the kitchen counter as I was "going down with the ship." I still rub that divot in the back of my head when I get the itch. Some of you may know what the itch is. For those of you that do not know, here's an idea.

For those of you that are shoppers—think Black Friday, the day after Thanksgiving. At what point do you start the countdown to getting ready to get up at 5:00 a.m. and plan your route aisle to aisle?

And those who aren't shoppers? At what point do you start your countdown for your shopper to leave?

Wherever We Go, There We Are

There you go . . .

So, this seems like a good stopping point. You get the idea and extent of my pill use. I was able to sober up in ICU, again, and then transfer to a residential treatment for men. Funny thing is, when I get there, all I see are boys. Including me. I have never seen so many adult children whine and bicker about so many petty things in my entire life! Phone use, cigarettes, television time, clothes, food . . . and on and on.

Lemme break it down for you outsiders. I'm considered a "professional retread" in these centers. Once we get out of detox and are clear of danger levels of booze or benzos or such, they say, "You need further help. We have a 30-day men's center in the middle of nowhere where you can focus in total recovery."

So now you are in this big dorm house meeting guys from all walks of life. You got the high-end addict, the low-end addict, the unsure addict, and my favorite, the vacation addict. He is the one who will be king of the boys. Now please guys and gals who are reading this who went to a center, shhhh. Wait. I'm getting there.

As in every medical journal or video or book known to man, when a person starts the addiction, their mental level stops growing. So, we sober up and are left with a 5'10 14-year-old. Ergo, a boy. After 30 days of sobriety, we feel invincible and ready for the world. We are men and women! No, no we're not. Not yet, that is. The growth has just begun. The centers are designed to hopefully guide you and me and nurture us to go into the world, knowing there will be dangers and challenges. We grow and learn from the past and knowledge about the now. When you do things right, people will think you did nothing at all. And there it is, plain and simple. Even a crappy center can help you if you are willing to put forth the work, and never quit trying. You quit, you fail.

It wasn't immediate for me. But years later, while enjoying the silence on Lake LBJ, Texas, a powerful realization overcame me, "When I am completely sober, I am not so much an asshole as I am drunk or high."

To me, this was a revelation. Other addicts out there will feel different about this and their own awakening. As they should. But in my life, to realize this situation was a wake-up call! So, what to do now?

The Deadly Combination

I was pretty sure smoking cocaine and drinking scotch wasn't in this equation. To use, or not to use. That is the question. But here's the problem. I loved to drink. Seriously, I loved it. I loved the ritual of buying it, mixing the perfect ratio of scotch to ice, I loved the effects it produced. Then when I'm good and drunk, the urge to smoke crack kicks in and once again, Wesley and the Devil are off playing in "to hell with you" land.

Being a thinker, all those quotes and sayings I've heard all my life and in AA started to make sense and become annoying. My favorite ones were, "What are you willing to do to stay sober today?" and "Are you gonna cut bait? Or fish?"

So, I fished. I quit the booze and at first, it was so I wouldn't do any coke. Then, over time as my head, spirit, and memory started to clear, it was for the happiness. And today I am.

I have put together a new life, an amount of sobriety, and gained energy and a drive. Sure, I could stand to lose a few pounds around the middle, but one thing at a time. But even with that challenge, I love who I am today.

What is it we know about our drug of choice? Well, for the most part, more than half of the drunks and addicts I have met over the last 20 years started off with a single addiction. This would be what society has labeled as a "gateway" drug. Eh, they're right. Mine was booze. Others may have chosen weed, pills, coke, or gone right to the forbidden—heroin. At some point in our magnetic personality called life, we are introduced. Then it progresses to something better, something stronger . . . all the while pollinating the addiction to cross over. And when that drug is dried up and no longer available, we move onto a new drug. And so on, and so on. Like my brothers and sisters in the program, I am what doctors call a polysubstance abuser. Means I like a lot of things that'll get me high. Oh, and I didn't mean all my bros and sisses were like me. An overwhelming majority of us will focus on a single addiction without ever knowing or wanting to try anything else. I just hit the trifecta in my own life.

If by the means of a miracle from God Himself we don't die from an overdose, and He sees fit to keep our grungy butts on this rock a little longer, then it's time for help. Treatment. If you have someone, anyone, in your family who is even remotely willing to help you, let alone listen to you ask for help, love that person for being there with you in the beginning process of recovery. I swear, one day you both will look back and laugh (pssst—if you stay sober).

The healing begins when the student is beaten. Hopefully in treatment we are honest from the get go. Talk about cross-addiction and possible dual diagnosis shit. The more you get out, the better the chance for survival you got.

So now in recovery, we talk about why we do what we do. We talk about feelings and journal and go to meetings . . . A lot of meetings all day every day. Granted, it isn't always a peaceful experience while getting sober. Sometimes there are factors that we have that just can't seem to get out of the way. Keep in mind our body, mind, and spirit have only been chemical free up to 30 days and our brains are trying to reboot. It is going to take time. So everyone just be patient. When you start feeling like you're out of whack, remember this:

Stay calm

Control your breathing

Call someone who will listen

Realize it's only temporary

Don't do what I did.

What I would do when my demons would surface is start with the scotch. My head would be swimming so fast with thoughts of misery, despair, and gloom, I couldn't drink fast enough to make the thoughts go away. But with each next drink, my mind would slowly forget the chaos circling around in my melon.

I knew drinking would help with the noises, but I also knew there would be consequences after the numbing effect went away. Either way, I just did not care.

More than half of the time, the alcohol itself would not make the memories go away, just intensify them. So then the next step for me was to get cocaine. Having a completely numb brain would do the trick and take away the pain. And it did . . . as long as I had the money to back up my supply. And when the money was gone and the powder or crack was all used up, the guilt, shame, cravings, and problems all came back. Ergo, the cycle continued to go around and around. I continued to get sicker and sicker.

CHAPTER 8
SWITCH HITTING—ONE ADDICTION FOR ANOTHER

My addiction didn't start with drinking. This is so true for so many of us. Reflecting on my youth, I now see there were some warning signs that a therapist nor anyone not "like me" would ever see. Here's a quick few: Compulsion to spend money, sitting in front of the television to escape, selling personal items below cost... yea, I know, an eighth-grade pawn broker and client. This was ever so present in the junior high years.

In today's society with television the way it is, it makes my behavior almost acceptable. But either then or now, it is not normal nor sane behavior. I was hustling and dealing by the spring of my eighth-grade year. My poison... marbles. I could sell marbles to a snake. I was that good. I had no idea I was sharpening my sales technique and sales pitch for my future. See? Education does me good. So, I never stopped learning. And I got creative. Sometimes it was marbles, then it went to baseball cards. It went into the wide world of comic books too. But now that I think back, my favorite was painting and cutting up brown paper shopping bags and wearing them on the street dancing for money... er, change.

John R and I had a great time doing stuff like that. At least I can say at that point it was comical and juvenile but not drug or alcohol induced. Eventually over time it did get to that point and I lost my friend to my idiotic choices. And the next thing I knew, he's out of my mind and I'm on to the next life to ruin. And then the next. Then another one. And so on, and on, and on. All for the rush. I honestly believe this was my addiction acting out in the only way it knew how.

Over the years, I have witnessed friends and associates in life and in recovery do this. Nonsmokers become smokers, healthy bodies became fat bodies. Still others became shopaholics and even sex addicts. Not one of them had any intention of doing what they did. It was the fact that their main drug of choice was no longer a part of their routine. And I, definitely falling into a group category, did the same thing. Seems we were doing what only felt natural. Like breathing.

And this part, my friends, has gotta be my favorite. I've said it thousands of times, and also have heard it from others in and out of recovery. God, I love this. Ready? If you have done this too, say the following out loud: "As long as I'm not (fill in blank), what I'm doing is okay." Now, if after reading that and you can relate, look around and see if that statement is true. If it is, stop and change life's direction. If it isn't, do what you do.

But switching can be just as dangerous. At least in my life. I know two things, (A) I can only work on me, and (B) no rules, no pants! Both are great to live by. One to try and better myself, and the other to remember to laugh. It's gotten me through multiple overdoses, a head wound, cancer, a hernia, an assault from an armed guard, alcohol poisoning, depression, mania, insomnia, detoxing, poverty, riches, marriage, and so much shame. Just remember to laugh one joke at a time.

Anyway, that we can better ourselves in any aspect of our lives shows hope. Because unless we take action to recognize our wrongs after sobriety, we can still dig a deeper hole for ourselves. It boils down to nature. More specifically, my addictive nature. We all have it. Some are stronger than others but we have it. So, since we are talking about me, let's do just that.

My addictive nature states: If I invest any amount of time in to something, my nature kicks in and then it's followed by the compulsion and desire to consume/control/suffocate. I was watching a documentary about a man who quit drinking, and from what I understood, he drank a lot, a whole lot. Never again to drink another drop, he went on with his life. In which he inadvertently became a hoarder. I saw filth and grime everywhere. Stuff he collected was not even important on any level. He believed that what he was doing was okay and not harming anyone. Germs, bacteria, and spores took over his body. And since his previous career was alcoholism, his health and immune system had been compromised and if not treated, he will most likely die.

We are the blindest when it comes to our own addiction and post-addiction. Believe that. The minute we open our mouths to defend our own actions in addiction, the shit starts to fly out of everywhere.

We think we either have our lives and challenges under control, or flat out just do not care. Some of us will live like this for the rest of our life. Others will die, one by one; those who don't, will go to jail. Once again proving, wherever we go, there we are. What would it take for you, me, or the guy sitting on the bench to get sober and on track? Addicts are not afraid of pretty much anything. It may seem like it when we are in the crosshairs, but think about it. Guys and dolls, how many times did we still drink and get behind the wheel? Or smoke that joint and still show up to the probation department knowing there was a chance of a piss test? Or stay out using all night, then return home to our loved ones with a story of why we don't have the rent money? See? Not afraid of anything. And now that we've gone over the line into cross-addiction, we are now being creative with our stories and "on cue" crying. Just like anything else, it is going to take some serious time to get everything in check.

It took a good 15 plus years for me to get it. It was a revolving door for me. I managed some sober time in between all the lapses. Everyone had an idea how I was to live my life but me. And for the benefit of the doubt, I tried every suggestion given.

I gained an incredible amount of knowledge from my experiences, and some great stories for future books and for gatherings with close friends and newcomers. I also learned to have structure within to lead a good life. And today I do just that. It's really 80% listening. Over the years, I have met hundreds, and possibly thousands, of men and women who at some point have flat out said they have cross-addiction and what do they do. Most of the time after I listen to them talk out loud, they find their answer. Not from my responses, but by simply bouncing their thoughts off of someone who listens. You may have problems of every size and shape when you begin the road to revelation, but once you are on it, they melt away to challenges. And everyone can handle a challenge.

Plants, humans, and animals need nourishment to survive. And as you know, this can be both easy and hard. But with work and proper communicational care, we survive to grow up and be a burden on the census market. Challenges are the same thing. A little or a lot of work, some communication and time and whammo—a resolution has been found.

Sharing stories, experiences, and information in the recovering community is like housewives swapping recipes—everyone just wants the right ingredients to make it better. Some of what I heard was exciting, I ain't gonna lie. Some of it was sad and a learning experience. But I took what I needed and left the rest. The same should go for you. I've learned one thing—you have to find your own path. There are a lot of signs and wisdom on the path, hence take the obvious. But always remember that it is your path. Some take a road which few do, and others follow a worn trail. Either way, both lead to the answers.

My answers may not be your answers. And yours won't be the right ones for the next new guy or gal. But you share one story, and you help pave a starting point for them to start the walk.

CHAPTER 9
STUCK IN A FUNK

I had a lot of motivation when I started the program of recovery. Watching drunks and addicts talk and laugh and still have money in their pockets gave me hope. I was new. I had a fresh pair of eyes. I knew anything these guys were doing was better than whatever I was doing. Darkness became light, misery turned into hope, failure became motivation to do better and desire finally took over and transformed hopelessness. And this feeling was addictive as well.

At this point in my life, I thought it was all about the drugs. By this, I mean I thought the way I was acting was based on my drug and alcohol intake. This is partially true. I did not know there was an underlying factor called depression or mania or bipolar which had been ignored and suppressed for many years. Once the initial detox is done, most of us will face this.

So once again, I got off the chemicals and my body was completely clean of them. I now had to face them, figure them out, and learn how to work through them.

I don't know what it was like for any of you out there, but for me it felt as if I was a kindergarten learning algebra. I was lost. My counselor would say stuff like, "How do you feel?" and things like, "Use 'I' statements." Not as easy as it sounds. The truth of the matter is I was raised in a different kind of structure—nothing said, nothing wrong.

Anyways, after years of therapy, medications, counseling, and AA, I realized I had reached a new level of happiness and contentment. As I grew, so did my family in Al-Anon. They were learning how to live for themselves.

I am proud, once again, to report my mother is a 4th degree blackbelt in Al-Anon. And I couldn't be more happier or proud of her.

At this level I was basking in, I discovered a new sense of peace. I was laughing and growing and accepting friends. Life as I knew it was good. But I was soon to learn that with the good, comes the bad.

My next life lesson: A funk is a funk is a funk. They happen to everyone. It won't discriminate between 1 day sober or 10 years sober. They happen!

Anxiety, depression, and rage would surface and stay dominate for weeks at a time. I began to think things like, "I'll never quite get this 'program' thing," or "If this is what sobriety brings, I don't want it," and even, "Why do I get so miserable even when I'm doing the right things?" Little did I know, time would tell all answers.

I honestly felt like no matter how hard I would try, I would never stay sober. Anyone else feel that way too? Poppa did not raise a quitter, so I sucked it up and got back into the arena. So here I am, scared and confused, trying to establish a fall-off point to begin my quest to figure out what to do when one of those funk sessions made itself known.

This meant I had to educate myself. My fall-off point began in Houston at a dual diagnosis meeting. This is a safe place that at first, may feel awkward to sit and listen to a story coming from another person who is describing your life to a T. I was no longer alone, and no longer the only one with a similar story I found unique and different. I was home and I was welcomed with open arms.

Next, I went to a psychiatrist who dealt specifically with "dual diagnosis." As in life, it was important for me not to hold back anything when telling my story. One never knows what others can pick up just from listening. There's always a detail within a detail.

Having now spent years in the program, it was easy for me to share my feelings and emotions as they came. Some say I am too open. Others say I don't speak enough. I say I speak what I need to in order to get the point across. One thing to add is to make sure you trust you doctor completely when opening up. If you don't, then by all means go get a new one. It's your life.

Some of us can go into the rooms of AA and get what they are saying and go off and "get it" the first time in. Others do not. This is my category.

It took me a long time. So, these are my brothers and sisters I am trying to reach in this chapter. For those of you that did get it the first time in, you spent your hard-earned money for this book so you might as well go ahead and read this chapter anyways. Then go and help a drunk in a funk that's feeling bunk!

As years came and went by, the anxiety and rage did go away. And underlying all that? More depression. So, when a funk came along, and depression rolled in like a Scottish fog, I did what all the depressed people do, I drank and I drugged, I wouldn't eat, and I slept 14 hours a day. Most of my friends not in the program would shrug and tell me to hang in there. And my AA family would tell me to pick up the Big Book and hit a meeting and all would be okay in God's hands. Pops would tell me to get active—walk, ride a bike, and so on—and exercise would take care of my mental health. All valid suggestions. But none would work.

Not this time anyways. But after one day, when the funk was clear and very in my face, I prayed for a miracle and got miracle whipped! Almost literally. I was going through the "poor me, poor me . . . pour me another drink" cycle when a reality hit me like a bat.

"No matter how happy or sober I will ever be, I am going to get depressed. Happiness ain't forever!"

It is a funky cycle. It is going to happen no matter what we do. Like buying food at the grocery store, eventually the food will run out and will have to be replaced. I always waited till my depression got really, really twisted before I would try to do anything about it. Now, I pause. When I'm feeling sad, pause.

The anger or irritability cycle, pause. Or even if I wanted to start my day over again, pause. Reverend Jim taught me this. AA says, "One day at a time," "Pause when agitated," and my favorite, "Easy does it." Add mine to the mix and all it does is make my choices to recover infinite. However it is done, I always find the answer I am looking for.

Funks are just a part of life. Every single day is not going to be puppies, smiles, and music. With the good comes the bad.

People who do not have any addiction, disorder, or disease are just as perceptible to have bad days too. No one is immune to depression. In fact, those who go through depression and never had a challenge with "isms" I have a tendency to feel more for than I do my own kind. At least we have our insanity of addiction to buffer the blow of sadness. Normals have to jump in waist deep, completely blind. And because we attend meetings and reach out, we are prone to react and/or respond quicker to fix the situation than say, a normal nonalcoholic. Let me make clear one thing though, I have seen old timers in AA have a challenge with getting out of a depressional funk. If it's bad, go the emergency room. Seriously. But I personally know some of these old timers who are—and I think they prefer—very miserable and depressed in recovery. These men and women forgot the mere basics and are a pain in my ass and others to be around.

You will be able to pick them out in no time at all. But you also will be able to find other old timers that will help you to the ends of the earth. We are human. We will make mistakes and try our hardest to correct them if we can.

Being in recovery is the first step to feeling better about who we are and what we are. My pops used to say, "If you don't like the way you are or the way you feel, what are you willing to change?" We each have our own answer. Do you like the way you look? Feel? Or carry yourself? If the answer is no . . . What are you gonna do about it?

CHAPTER 10

UNDOING THE WRONGS

In twelve-step programs, they highly suggest that we make amends at some point in our recovery. We have to undo our wrongs.

When I sit back and think about all of the people in my life that I have hurt because of my alcohol and drug use, I think, "Man, there's a lot of people I have hurt." Pretty big insight, eh? But in reality, I hurt a lot of people. A 20-year span in multiple cities, states, and bars leaves a pretty heavy slime trail. I know I cannot grow spiritually, emotionally, and mentally unless I take proper action to do so. First, I had to actively recognize that I had hurt people. I was completely blind and ignorant to people and their feelings outside my personal bubble space. No one was immune.

Once I sought treatment and started having sessions with my family, I learned of the damages I caused. And it was only the beginning. My eyes were finally opened and I could see the chaos and destruction unfold in front of me as my mother, father, and brother painted a portrait of my alcoholic wake.

Now it makes sense why no one wanted to be with me or around me during, or long after, my addiction lingered. Ha! I was an asshole. Still, when I think back, it makes my stomach churn what I thought, in my mind, was acceptable.

Some of you out there have either gone through this, in the middle of it, or just now are waking up to the realization that you too might be an asshole. Do not feel bad. This is completely normal to feel. If there is a light at the end of your tunnel, it is knowing you can stop the cycle whenever you make the decision to end it. The cycle, that is. Not your life. That's one big "game over" button I do not want to push. So, don't do it. It ain't always that bad the next day.

Over the last five plus years, I have made amends as they crop up, show up, and blow up. The time came when I had worked the steps every day, continued to do the deal, and lived under my sponsors' shadows long enough. Now, the Big Book says to do the amends in a certain way—their way. And in the beginning, I did. I wanted to do everything by the book. I was so nervous when I had my first face-to-face amends to do. I remember thinking that it was going to be some big played out movie scene in my head and that this amends was going to be just as dramatic and emotional as the one spinning around in my head. Needless to say, it was quite boring and easy to do. No hate, no loud shouting, and no one's blood was drawn. If anything, the opposite. They laughed and shook my hand and said, "All I ever wanted to do was see you get help. And you did." That was it. I worked myself up for nothing. My pops used to say, "The anticipation of something is usually worse than the act itself."

But, damnit, this is an action we have to take and need to do. It's not something that we can skip and expect to move forward in life or even grow. Evolution took control over time and AA's version of how to make amends mixed in with my own version gave birth to what I do today. You "thumpers" out there ... get over it. There IS more than one way. But as we know, what may work for me may not work as well for the next person. Please, please find your own direction.

Know what I fear the most? Fear of rejection is a bitch. Right now, did you think of relationship rejection? Amazing, our brains. Rejection is the goose egg I keep walking around. When I believe that I'm not going to hear the answer I specifically want, I will either not confront the issue or take the conversation in another direction. But fear will prevent me from fulfilling my part of the agreement with God. Over the years, I learned this: Rejection will happen, but it's how the rejection is handled that matters. If I choose to shut down and get run over by the wrongs I have committed, then I have to lie in that bed. If I change the way I look at the approach and just do it, then that same bed isn't half bad to lie in. All of this seems to be common knowledge.

But, show me an alcoholic who is common and I'll show you a shyster who won't go to hell.

Lemme tell you a story with a great example. Once I jumped too early into wanting to make amends. For some reason, we do this. Anyways, I called this person and went on to say I was sorry and that she had every right to be angry for what I had done. After it was all over, I asked if she would forgive me. She immediately said no, and that I was not to ever call her again. I hung up and almost instantly my attitude went from vulnerable to "That bitch!" at the least—I know first off I did everything wrong. With the obvious out of the way, see how I handled the rejection? I could not see it as A) a stepping stone or B) a chance to learn and grow from this experience, and the cold hard truth.

With time, patience, and determination I gained confidence and knowledge about how to properly administer a correct and meaningful apology and amends. For me, it wasn't about what I was willing to do. It became what I was going to do.

All I ever heard was—what are you willing to do? No one ever said—what are you going to do? Anybody can be willing 100% of the time, but that's all you are: willing. I see it as a limbo state of accomplishment. After many years of people pounding it and general recovery into my rotting brain, I had to go and figure it out. Since no one else was going to tell or ask me ever again how I was going to do this, I just flat out did it!

I started incorporating AA-based themes in my brain and added my own components, baked for 30 minutes in medium and presto! I got my own jump-off point and a new frame of mind about life. It wasn't very pretty at first, kinda like sex your first time. But I kept at it and never gave up. It would take time to mold and shape.

So now I had this new "frame of mind" thinking and I set out on a journey that started 5 years ago and will only end when I'm in a Cigar Box casket, 6 feet under. Admittedly, I still have a fear about contacting these people from my past. It is always going to be there, the fear. What's different is I used to let the fear control my life. Now, my life dictates what's to fear and not to fear as calmly as if I ripped one sitting on a vinyl recliner.

Basically, this means I want true happiness and a piece of mindless happiness—a clarity, if you will. When I finally talked to my group of friends who had performed a whole lot of amends, they told every single amend they made ended the same way: with inner peace and gratitude. It didn't matter in the end if someone told them to go to hell or shove their sobriety where the sun doesn't shine; they know they did their most sincere and absolute best to do the right thing. It is great when someone accepts the amends and all is forgiven. But when the other person is too hurt and cannot let go, the deed was done.

Their side of the street was clean. Wow. This concept was like a revelation in my head.

I have been blessed and lucky. Since I started over with this whole process of righting my wrongs, and now writing my wrongs, everyone else has been more forgiving and loving and supportive. I have been able to rekindle a few relationships. Sometimes, I will go out of my way to make an amends. I do this process by phone, face-to-face, emails, letters, and searching for someone on Facebook. God has a reason for people being in our lives.

Some to love, some to hate, and others to learn from. I love them all. They are what keep me alive. The Godster dictates how it is going to work—not me. Anymore.

By the time you are reading this book—whether bought or borrowed or stolen—I hopefully will have made amends to my ex-wife and parents. I purposely waited until the end of my list to talk with my family members. Partially out of fear, and partially out of growth. They were, and still are, tired of hearing "I'm sorry" come out of my mouth day after day, hour after hour.

These are the people with whom I have spent the most obvious time with and also that they know me inside and out. They know my patterns and can almost predict when and where I would relapse.

Now they don't worry so much. I stopped with the "I'm sorrys" and started doing the "I'm doing and living" thing. When you do things right, people will think you did nothing at all. Remember that.

Now, I'm sober and living brightly. I had to know my life would make the 180-degree turn and stay there. So far, so good.

So, why am I telling you this? Well one, I'm an idiot, and two, you need to know you are not alone. If you think you are the only one with thoughts like you have, or you drink alone in your bathroom in your tub with a blanket over you in fear of the ceiling falling on you . . . you are not alone. I mean, I never did that, but I guarantee someone did. Every day, I am just as susceptible to the disease as the next guy or gal. If I don't do recovery on some level each day, I will die.

My fears may be someone else's hope. The feelings and emotions I have inside are pure and real. I have never experienced happiness and sadness and euphoria on any level like this. If you want it, go get it. If not, it will be here waiting for you at the door.

Come in, boys, the water's fine.

CHAPTER 11
THE TRIFECTA–ADDICTION, BIPOLAR, AND CANCER

By 1990, I knew I had a problem with alcohol. In 1993, I was labeled an alcoholic. At the time, it really did not bother me nor did I even really care. I had made the decision to drink regardless. This "fun" led to two DWIs within a year.

Here's a fun fact: When we, as addicts, get into trouble, all of a sudden, we are willing to do whatever it takes to stay OUT of jail. We don't necessarily care too much about what may put us in. Fun, right?

So now, with this new fire to stay out of jail which was lit under my ass, I had to absorb what these people were saying in AA and in outpatient.

When you have a fuel-injected lifestyle, any spark given off will get you where you need to go.

And after 3 months of sobriety, 3 months of rules, and 3 months of pain, I was off racing around town drinking again. I was having the bartenders set two down for every one I was either drinking or had finished drinking. Could I still maintain the best of both my worlds? I wondered if I could actually pull it off. With people like my parents, friends, and counselor watching over me . . . could I? Well, I could not. I didn't know then what I now know today. People look at you differently than you look at yourself. Outside view looking in, per se. They can see change. And we can see one good looking person in the mirror. But as blind as I was, I went through it anyways.

I failed, and I failed miserably. It wasn't all bad in the scheme of two worlds. I was going to meetings and as a result I ended up listening and learning from others' stories. I actually retained information.

The Trifecta—Addiction, Bipolar, and Cancer

But it was soon after getting my education that my negative side caught up with me, passed me in the inside lane, and by the end of the race, I was drunk on the floor. The whole "Screw it!" attitude popped its ugly head and gram by gram I slowly brought back cocaine into my life. Now my world had spun out of control. My consumption grew, and my depression was boiling over. I could not face anyone at any time on any day. So, I hid. I hid in a bottle, a baggie, behind a dumpster, in a dumpster, or anywhere I thought no one would look for me. I wanted help. But I sincerely thought I was one of the few that would never stay sober. What else could go wrong?

That very question got its answer one evening while hanging at my folks' house. Again, I had a little over 3 months of sobriety at the time (notice a pattern?). I was outside on the phone, talking to my counselor about who knows what, when it turned from talk into yelling. Whatever he and I were talking about turned into an argument and then I went straight to rage. I was screaming at the top of my lungs, throwing patio furniture around, and crying uncontrollably. Thinking back, these emotions happened quite often. Anyways, he told my family that there might be more than meets the eye. So with his words spoken, I was to meet some specialized doctor who not only dealt with drunks, but drunks with psychological disorders . . . shut up, I ain't crazy.

After hours of testing and Rorschach pictures, I was now labeled bipolar. I seem to have a few labels on my trunk. Hmm. He went on to follow up and say that I was a dual diagnosis case and now I had to treat two problems.

I never felt so small or alone than I did that day. In my mind, I was the only one in the whole wide world with this type of condition. I didn't know back then how to turn my problems into challenges. Eventually, I would.

Next step was to seek out a psychiatrist. I found one and started my sessions almost immediately. Now I had to "share" all my feelings, frustrations, and anger with someone I didn't even know. Doc put me on medications and said to take them every day. I did. My thinking was that these medications would work like aspirin and kick in in 30 minutes or so. I did not know I had to wait a full month before the effects would start to take.

After 2 weeks, I started to double my intake. And when nothing still happened, I went back to drinking. Not a very smart choice I made there. Within days, I was raging and drunk.

After a long battle with trial and error, sobriety and lapses, shrink after shrink, I finally stabilized. I owe my sanity and laughter to a certain doctor in Austin. Thank you "Niles." Do what you do!

Now, being stabilized isn't as fun and stress free as one would think. At one point, I thought if I took the medications I would be level-headed all of the time. Not the case. What did happen was that I still felt every emotion and was able to sanely express them in a healthy way. When I was angry, I got angry.

When I was sad, I displayed signs of sadness. And so on, and so on. Get the picture? I was now able to steer away from extreme lows and maintain a level consciousness. With counseling, medications, and communication, I was evolving. Slowly.

Years went by, and sobriety came and went. But I never gave up. Pops used to say, "Practice winning every day. Even Sunday." So, by nature, if I did screw up, then I just got right back on the horse and tried again.

Life itself was pretty stagnant and cloudy. I wanted change in my life and so I prayed. I prayed for happiness and a good woman. God gave me a happy woman. She was full of life and dreams. I recall somewhere in this book I said something about addictive personalities and magnetic personalities. She was the colorful magnet, and I was the stainless steel refrigerator stocked with booze and hot wings! We were a perfect match.

I married this Irish lass and became the stepfather to three beautiful, smart, and wonderful children. Being with Kell was like no other experience. It was meant to be. I truly loved her.

But, me being what and who I was, my past would soon catch up to me. In no time, I was drinking heavily again. But the seed was planted, and as bad as my drinking got, I was changing—sorta evolving. And I was letting it.

You see, prior to my wife, I absolutely did not want to have any restrictions, commitments, or responsibilities. I wanted to drink how much I wanted, and when I wanted. I also wanted to use as many drugs as I could without having a daily schedule. I knew I wanted to die by means of alcohol. And I welcomed it.

But my wife, most likely without her knowledge, had a purpose. And she enforced it. So I had to adapt to a lifestyle of drinking and fatherhood and being a husband. I wish I could say that my plan was well thought out and that I was able to balance all three. So, I won't.

I still tell Kell, to this day, that she is the one that saved my life. She will deny it, but she did. Then, with God's blessing, she gave birth to my daughter, my Bethany.

I have never experienced love and happiness the way I was always meant to experience. It is like trying to describe a new color.

Unless you have seen the color, you just don't have the words to describe it.

Now fast forward four years. After four years of drinking, drugging, car wrecks, and multiple overdoses, she had had enough and finally asked for a divorce. I would have divorced my ass too if I could have.

The depression was horrible. It took two-and-a-half years to get back to a leveled par. When I did, life was only tolerable.

I had a good job at the time and was sober. So now that I was finally stable and managing my alcoholism and mental health, I was acceptable to finally take that deep breath we do and feel that life itself was going to be okay.

In the middle of December of that same year, I went to work as always and soon I began to throw up. Not uncommon for me, but physically something was wrong. Throwing up some blood is always a good sign. So, I went to the emergency room and the doctor ran test after test. Guess there was a BMW somewhere that needed a car payment. After an almost full 24-hours, a doctor I hadn't met yet came into my room and informed me of the cancer on my right kidney. Everything I thought I knew and felt went right out the window. My heart stopped, and all that blood went to the bottom of my feet. I broke into tears and hysteria. The only thought running through my not-so-thick skull was, "What in His name am I going to do and what will happen to Bethy?"

In a brief moment of clarity, I somehow managed to call my father in Houston. I told him I was in the hospital and his response, like so many times before, was, "What's wrong THIS time?" I half blurted out and half sniffled that I had cancer. Then there was what seemed an eternity of silence. But actually, it was about five seconds in which he finally said, "I'll be there in an hour and ten minutes." Being in Austin, I know the trip takes about two hours. He made it in 90 minutes.

My brain was swimming in a pool of despair, and my depression was unbearable. My pops stuck with me the whole journey. But I will come back to that later. Having my dad there at the time was helpful. He is a "man with a plan" kind of guy. So, to him, the next step would be to self-inform ourselves with everything there was to know about kidney cancer. Off to the World Wide Web!

During the whole researching process, my will to prevent depression was sinking quicker and quicker. I even quit taking my medications for a month. My dad had to go back to Houston since that is where his life, wife, and other world is. Again, I was alone. And with this depression and loneliness, anger was born.

This was God's fault. And for that, I blamed Him. How? I got piss drunk constantly, waved my hand in the air, and cursed all that He had created. But knowing I was a dead man anyways, I drank and lived my life as if I would be dead in a month. The consumption was extravagant enough to get me into trouble with the law twice before the end of that same year. I raked in four citations: speeding, public intoxication, public lewdness, and drug paraphernalia. So back to the rooms of AA I went.

I told very few about my condition. Not because everyone would want to know where, when, how, and what they could do to help, but because Christmas was a week away and I could not handle being the center of attention. The ones I did tell were of course concerned and asked questions. But being drunks in recovery, the majority never followed up with my condition.

Not their fault. When you are in AA, you always have a full plate and sometimes other people's challenges are just that—other people's challenges.

In my own mind and world, I was a helpless victim and the only one in the world with cancer. Keep in mind at the time I was completely blind to reality, okay? But during my research, I started to look at websites that dealt with cancer survivors and I found out there are a lot of people like me out there.

Some of the stories were not as bad as mine, still others had it so much worse than me. And the cruelest of them all were the children with cancer. These boys and girls are the bravest of us all. What a selfish, self-absorbed bastard I was. My heart went out to them. It still does.

The Trifecta—Addiction, Bipolar, and Cancer

My whole outlook toward my own situation took a 180-degree turn and I saw that I could get through this. A flame of hope began to come to life within me.

The only stipulation I had about the removal of my cancer was that it would have to be done before the Super Bowl. My favorite team, the Pittsburg Steelers, was about to whoop up on the Arizona Cardinals, and I did not want to be hospitalized during this event. I got my way, and on January 27, 2009, at 7:00 a.m., they took out the cancer along with a third of my kidney. I recovered on my parents' couch while watching the Steelers win a nail-biting victory over Arizona. I almost tore out my staples when they won their sixth ring. God, they rock!

Most of the time, a doctor will tell you what to expect after having a major surgery or having a major organ partially removed. Not in this case. My body was going through chemical changes I was not aware of. As a result, I was feeling different. To be more specific, I became psychotically depressed. I lost the will to function, eat, work, or live.

So, I once again did what I so often would do—I drank. And in March of that year, I earned yet another DWI. But I did not care. In my head I was already trying to figure out a way to kill myself. Now, I thought, I would have to do it in jail. Or find someone inside to do it for me. As fate would have it, I was released on a personal bond and thrown back into the world. I white knuckled my sobriety for the next 3 months and was institutionalized twice for depression and suicidal thoughts and actions. I was at the point where I believed I was going to spend the rest of my life wearing pajamas and bouncing around a rubber room. It would not be until September before a prayer, any prayer, would be answered.

The ninth month rolled around and I was scheduled to visit my daughter and ex-wife for a weekend. Up until the day before, I was in a horrible depression and could not do anything but lie in bed and stare at the ceiling. My only sense of happiness was knowing I was about to see my daughter. So, lying in bed, I talked to God. I talked of pain, sadness, and depression. I did the only thing I knew to do at the time . . . I prayed. I prayed for change and the ability to simply smile again.

At 6:00 a.m., I left Austin and headed south to see my little girl. While driving, I watched the sun rise over the Hill Country for the first time sober in a loooong time. It was pretty darn cool. When I got to Kell's house, I was thrown into family life.

Bethy was running for class council and needed poster board signs for election slogans. You know, "Vote for Bethany, it's your destiny!" stuff like that. I was able to get out of my own dark world and step into a bright future known as kids.

It was incredibly awesome. I had stopped thinking about my own situation and started thinking of family. I haven't stopped smiling since. She won class president by the way. My heart changed. My life changed, and I stayed sober this time.

It seems like a country record you play backward: the kids come back, my ex likes me now, and I believe there is hope once again. That was 3 years ago. Life is good. I still deal with cancer follow-up treatments and life as it comes; I always need to remember I cannot get complacent. I have to have commitment in everything that I do.

Life still moves forward. I have seen friends die and jailed. I still have a crap load of wrongs I need to right, but I still "pause" and deal with them one at a time. Every day I go to bed sober is another reason to find gratitude in any challenge thrown at me that doesn't result in drinking or smoking cocaine.

My prayer was answered. Yours will be too. Never quit pushing forward and follow your heart. It has taken me a third of my life to get where I am. Sometimes it can be quickly, and other times it can take forever. But you will get there. Because remember, wherever we go, there we are. And what are you going to do when you get there?

CHAPTER 12
THE LAST CHAPTER

"It's the journey, not the destination"

Well, like most great stories and heartwarming movies, we have to come to the end. I have composed five years' worth of notes and a lifetime of experience into this book hoping it may reach and help at least one person. There are still two things I would like to share with y'all that has made an impression and helped me to look at the big picture I call life.

There once was an experiment done to see if anyone in society would notice a "No Name" type of person with an extraordinary talent. They hired a world class musician who plays the violin. They gave him an expensive violin and placed him at a major train station stairwell exit where people would have to pass him and have to take notice. Supposedly, it was one of the busiest on and off stations in the area. So this musician stood in the middle of all these buzzing people and played the most beautiful music composed by Mozart and others. Apparently, no one formed any type of gathering around him nor did anyone stop to listen. More than 1,000 people walked by.[1]

So, the question is, if the violinist was a somebody standing there, would anyone notice or care?

This experiment got me thinking about us addicts, alcoholics, and people who are witnessing our recovery. When we sober up, do people notice? All answers point to yes. Do they notice also when we choose not to sober up or relapse? Again, yes. No matter what we do, people ARE going to notice and have an opinion. They may not stop and say something to us, but they sure as hell will talk to everyone else.

So, when we do sober up, they may say things like, "Oooh, you look so different," or "Good for you!" Other times it may not be so nice. They may say, and I can testify to this, things like, "You may be sober now, but you'll go back." Most people will be happy when we stop our insanity. Still, others won't. The point is that no matter what we do, people will be watching. As we know, we are unable to control what our friends and family will think nor can we control their outlook. We can only control our own actions, thoughts, and feelings. Maybe in time and technology, we will have a device to control others and their way of thinking. I'd use it to make lawyers and judges fight each other MMA style. Sweeeeeet!

For me, when someone I know says, "It's good to see you," I return with, "It's good to be seen." In saying this out loud, it puts me out there with a sense of accountability to continue to be seen. I need to be noticed whether it is reflected in a positive or negative behavior. Either one is a form and possibility for growth. For the most part, I have been lucky with the feedback from others.

People also notice when we "bug out" and sink into our active addiction and this is apparent when they start shaking their heads when we do what we do. Respectfully, most of the time they will nod their heads in agreement when we stop using and start re-recovering. I mean, who doesn't want to be a new man or woman. Do you?

Good luck, God bless, and groovy recovery! And now for your enjoyment...pictures!

Wesley and Mitch: two creative Imagineers

No one thought I could touch my brain

There is no hiding how trashed I am

Wesley and Austin out looking for trouble

Why so serious?

Just an idiot in between writing chapters

Practicing for a mug shot

I am what I am

DON'T YOU GO ANYWHERE!!!!!!! YAKITY YAK, THERE'S MORE HERE IN THE BACK...

As an added bonus, this next "writing" was created three days after the diagnosis of the "C word." Without the support and bully-style parenting, I do not think I would have made it in this life. Appreciate what you have in life, people. A father's love may be quiet, but it carries a big punch.

PHILOSOPHY ACCORDING TO DICK
BY
WESLEY BRANN

50 of the Best Quotes

Growing up, my father—Richard Brann—had a quote for pretty much any situation you can think of. Some of these I kept because they were important to me in my development. Others, I threw to the curb as if they were spoken from a wild man. But every single one of them I accepted and at least tried. Some of the stuff you will read comes from history itself. This man would sell the clothes off his back if it would help another human being. He is my role model, my amigo, and my father... So shut your mouth, sit back, and enjoy the hell out of my book!

"WHEREVER YOU GO, THERE YOU ARE!"

"IF YOU TAKE CARE OF YOUR CAR, YOUR CAR WILL TAKE CARE OF YOU."

"NEVER STOP LEARNING!"

"PRACTICE WINNING EVERY DAY."

"THIS INFORMATION I HAVE FOR YOU ON MAINTAINING YOUR HEALTH IS SO VERY IMPORTANT. SO WHATEVER YOU DO, DON'T READ IT!"

"EVERYTHING IN LIFE CAN BE SOLVED WITH TIME, PATIENCE, AND PERSEVERANCE."

"WHEN ALL ELSE FAILS, FOLLOW INSTRUCTIONS."

"YOU'RE AS MUCH HELP AS A ONE-LEGGED MAN IN A BUTT-KICKING CONTEST!"

"POOR ME, POOR ME, POUR ME ANOTHER DRINK."

"EVERY TIME I COME HERE, I FEEL LIKE I'VE BEEN HERE BEFORE."

"SUM QUOD ERIS." (I AM WHAT YOU SHALL BE)

"*TEMPEST FEUGET!*" (TIME FLIES)

"AS LONG AS I TAKE THESE VITAMINS HERE, I WILL NEVER DIE. SO YOU GOT THAT TO LOOK FORWARD TO."

"KIDNEY STONES AREN'T AS MUCH FUN AS YOU WOULD THINK THEY ARE."

"NEVER ASK A FAT LADY ON AN ELEVATOR WHEN HER BABY IS DUE."

"IF YOU USED HALF THE TIME YOU DO WATCHING TV, AND INVESTED IT IN YOUR SCHOOLWORK, YOU JUST MAY GRADUATE."

"IF YOU WOULD QUIT SMOKING, I WOULDN'T HAVE TO WORRY ABOUT YOU GETTING CANCER AGAIN."

"ALWAYS TAKE TIME FOR YOURSELF. LEARN TO PACE 'CAUSE LIFE AIN'T A RACE. BECAUSE IN THE END, THE ONLY WAY TO WIN IS TO DIE."

"NEVER LET YOUR CHECKING ACCOUNT GO BELOW $50.00."

"MAKE A LIST EVERY MORNING TO SEE WHAT YOU WOULD LIKE TO HAVE ACCOMPLISHED BY THE END OF THE DAY."

"YOU GOTTA START OFF EACH DAY WITH A SONG . . .
EVEN IF THINGS ARE WRONG."

"EVERYBODY AT SOME POINT IN THEIR LIVES ARE GONNA WANT FREE LEGAL ADVICE."

"IT'S MY JOB TO BE WORRIED SICK ABOUT YOU!"

"YOU'RE NOT SO MUCH OF A DUMB ASS AS I THOUGHT YOU'D BE."

"WHAT DOES NOT KILL YOU WILL ONLY MAKE YOU STRONGER!"

"COLD COFFEE MAKES ME BEAUTIFUL!"

"SOMETIMES, I DON'T KNOW WHETHER TO HUG YOU OR PUNCH YOU IN THE FACE!"

"YOU GET OUTTA LIFE WHAT YOU THINK YOU PUT IN."

"IT'S A NICE NIGHT FOR AN EVENING!"

"IF YOU HAVE A LARGE ELEPHANT IN FRONT OF YOU ON A LARGE PLATE, YOU HAVE TO EAT IT ALL ONE SMALL BITE AT A TIME."

"IF YOU PUT YOUR EAR TO THE GROUND AND YOUR NOSE TO THE GRIND STONE, SOONER OR LATER YOU'LL GET ADMITTED."

"GNARLY BOGUS!" (A COMMON PHRASE SAID IN THE MIDDLE OF EXCITEMENT OR BOREDOM)

"ALWAYS BE POLITE TO OTHERS."

"DON'T BUG YOUR BOSS. YOU MIGHT GET A CHANCE TO LEAVE EARLY AGAINST YOUR WILL."

"ACCOMPLISH EVERYTHING YOU WANT OVER A LONG PERIOD OF TIME."

"BE RESPONSIBLE FOR YOURSELF."

"MAKE FRIENDS WHEREVER YOU GO."

"YOUR LAZINESS REFLECTS EVERYTHING YOU ACCOMPLISH."

"YOU NEVER GET A SECOND CHANCE TO MAKE A FIRST IMPRESSION."

"WOOKIE JOOKIE, JOOKIE!" (I HAVE NO IDEA ON THIS ONE. IT'S BEEN SAID SO MANY TIMES OVER THE YEARS, IT STUCK)

"NO MATTER WHAT YOU DO IN LIFE OR PATH YOU TAKE,
I WILL ALWAYS BE PROUD OF YOU!"

"EVEN BEFORE WE KNEW WE WERE GOING TO ADOPT YOU, I KNEW YOU WOULD ALWAYS BE MY SON."

"A DRUNK MAN'S WORDS ARE ALSO A SOBER MAN'S THOUGHTS."

"WHATEVER YOU DO IN LIFE, DO IT 100%."

"IT AIN'T AS BAD AS YOU THINK. IT WILL LOOK BETTER IN THE MORNING!" –GEN. COLIN POWELL

"GET MAD, THEN GET OVER IT." -GEN. COLIN POWELL

"BE CAREFUL WHAT YOU CHOOSE. YOU MAY GET IT."
-GEN. COLIN POWELL

"DON'T LET ADVERSE FACTS STAND IN THE WAY OF A GOOD DECISION." -GEN. COLIN POWELL

"YOU CAN'T MAKE SOMEONE ELSE'S CHOICES. YOU SHOULDN'T LET SOMEONE ELSE MAKE YOURS." -GEN. COLIN POWELL

"SHARE CREDIT." -GEN. COLIN POWELL

(Those last quotes are from my father's mouth. But because they originally come from such an incredible military leader, we have those quotes printed out and posted on the side of the fridge. If ever we had a challenge we were stuck in, the list was used often. I just wanted to give a tribute to the man I would call Dad if my pops ever kicked the bucket: Gen. Colin Powell.)

THE END!

"ME, MYSELF, & ABOUT I"
A BIOGRAPHY TRAILER

I was born a poor little Eskimo boy from Nashville. Wait, this isn't the one I'm getting paid to do for that guy, is it? No? Okay then. I was born in 1972 in Houston, Texas, to a beautiful and giving mother, a beautiful mother who accepts me and loves me the same.

I schooled in the local area until freshman year of high school, when I went from a public life to a military-school life. Being who I am, an adaption was easily made and life began to be a lot more interesting. From there, I tried a couple of colleges, but both turned out to be liars and butt clenchers. Ergo, I write today. In fact, I wrote all the time growing up and through college, then nothing serious till now.

But a dear and sweet friend of mine, Marla Trevino, uncovered some of the writings I did in high school during my dark, "Clive Barker" days. Thank you. I can now share it, revised, with the public. (Ya know, let people know I can write a variety of mind-altering stuff.) Drugs, my control, and depression crept into my life and took me for a 26-year ride. And in that time, I got married to the love of my life, raised three beautiful children, as Kelli would say, and a mini-me of our own. Bethy is the reason for my seasons.

My life is a movie waiting to be never made. But I don't care about those kind of things. I write to express the beauty of words—words that sing on. Drugs and cancer and scotch and myself tried to kill me. But here I am.

NOTES

Chapter 1: The Educational Part
1. *Nosferatu*, directed by F. W. Murnau (1922: Jofa-Atelier, Berlin-Johannisthal).
2. "*Was ihn nicht umbringt, macht ihn starker,*" Friedrich Nietzsche, *Twilight of the Idols* (Leipzig: 1889).

Chapter 2: Crazy Does It
1. Paraphrased from *The Simpsons*, "Whacking Day," (April 29, 1993: Season 4, episode 20).

Chapter 4: Admitted
1. References made in this book to the Big Book of Alcoholics Anonymous are made with entire respect and recognition. The B.B. works, people, just use it as a guide to show you how to live! Give it to someone who isn't an addict and they will see that it's a new way of life. Watch B.B. studies that thump and preach and stay clear.
2. *Dracula*, directed by Tod Browning (1931: Universal Studios, CA).

Chapter 12: The Last Chapter
1. "The Time When Joshua Bell Went Busking, But No-One Cared," *ClassicFM*, September 17, 2014, http://www.classicfm.com/artists/joshua-bell/guides/busking-subway.

www.ingramcontent.com/pod-product-compliance
Lightning Source LLC
LaVergne TN
LVHW051523070426
835507LV00023B/3261